GOODSON MUMBA

Mindful Management

Harnessing the Power of Neurolinguistic in Management

Copyright © 2024 by Goodson Mumba

All rights reserved. No part of this publication may be reproduced, stored or transmitted in any form or by any means, electronic, mechanical, photocopying, recording, scanning, or otherwise without written permission from the publisher. It is illegal to copy this book, post it to a website, or distribute it by any other means without permission.

First edition

ISBN: 9798335329248

This book was professionally typeset on Reedsy. Find out more at reedsy.com

Contents

Preface — iv
Acknowledgement — vi
Dedication — vii
Disclaimer — viii

1. Chapter 1: Introduction to Mindful Management — 1
2. Chapter 2: Foundations of Neurolinguistic — 8
3. Chapter 3: Leadership Communication and Influence — 14
4. Chapter 4: Motivation and Goal Setting — 21
5. Chapter 5: Conflict Resolution and Negotiation — 28
6. Chapter 6: Emotional Intelligence and Self-Awareness — 36
7. Chapter 7: Mindful Decision Making — 44
8. Chapter 8: Performance Feedback and Coaching — 52
9. Chapter 9: Team Dynamics and Collaboration — 60
10. Chapter 10: Change Management and Adaptability — 68
11. Chapter 11: Creativity and Innovation — 74
12. Chapter 12: Cultural Sensitivity and Diversity — 80
13. Chapter 13: Stress Management and Well-being — 87
14. Chapter 14: Ethical Leadership and Integrity — 93
15. Chapter 15: Future Trends and Applications — 99

About the Author — 106

Preface

In today's fast-paced and ever-evolving business landscape, the role of effective leadership and management practices cannot be overstated. As organizations navigate complex challenges and strive for sustainable success, it becomes increasingly essential for leaders to cultivate a deep understanding of human behavior, communication dynamics, and cognitive processes.

In this book, "Mindful Management: Harnessing the Power of Neurolinguistics in Management," we embark on a transformative journey into the intersection of mindfulness, leadership, and neurolinguistics. Drawing upon cutting-edge research and practical insights, we explore how the principles of neurolinguistics can be harnessed to enhance leadership effectiveness, foster employee engagement, and drive organizational success.

Through a series of comprehensive chapters, we delve into the fundamental concepts of neurolinguistics, exploring its applications in leadership communication, motivation, conflict resolution, emotional intelligence, decision-making, and more. Each chapter offers a deep dive into the theoretical underpinnings of neurolinguistics, accompanied by real-world examples, practical strategies, and actionable techniques for applying these principles in managerial contexts.

As we journey through these pages, we invite you to explore the transformative power of neurolinguistics in management, and to discover how mindfulness and linguistic awareness can revolutionize the way you lead, communicate, and inspire others. Whether you are a seasoned executive, a budding entrepreneur, or a frontline manager, this book offers invaluable insights and tools to help you navigate the complexities of modern leadership with clarity, compassion, and effectiveness.

We are honored to accompany you on this journey of discovery and growth, and we hope that the insights shared in these pages will empower you to become a more mindful, empathetic, and impactful leader in your organization and beyond.

Warm regards,

Goodson Mumba

Acknowledgement

I would like to eternally and gratefully acknowledge the Almighty God for the infinite intelligence from His universal mind where we draw from all that we come to know and are yet to know. May I also acknowledge and thank everyone that has played a part in my journey of life in terms of spiritual, moral, emotional and material support.

Dedication

I extend my sincerest gratitude to my beloved wife, Edith Mumba, and our children, Angelina, Lubuto, Letticia, Lulumbi, and Butusho, for their unwavering support and understanding throughout the conception, writing, and eventual publication of this book, despite the sacrifices and challenges they endured.

Disclaimer

This book is a work of fiction. Names, characters, businesses, places, events, and incidents are either the products of the author's imagination or used in a fictitious manner. Any resemblance to actual persons, living or dead, or actual events is purely coincidental.

1

Chapter 1: Introduction to Mindful Management

"Awakening Leadership: The Journey Begins"

Jonathan sat in his spacious corner office, his brow furrowed with concern as he glanced over the latest quarterly report. Despite the company's impressive growth, he couldn't shake the feeling of unease gnawing at him. The relentless demands of the business world had taken their toll, leaving him feeling disconnected from his team and unsure of his own leadership abilities.

One morning, as Jonathan pondered his next move, a knock on his door interrupted his thoughts. It was Sarah, his trusted executive assistant, with an envelope in hand.

"Jonathan, this just arrived for you," Sarah said, her voice tinged with curiosity. "It's from Dr. Elizabeth Summers."

Jonathan's interest piqued at the mention of Dr. Summers, a renowned expert in neurolinguistics whose work he had admired from afar. With a sense of anticipation, he opened the envelope to find an invitation to attend a workshop on "Mindful Management: Harnessing the Power of Neurolinguistics."

Intrigued by the prospect of a fresh perspective, Jonathan decided to accept the invitation. Little did he know, this decision would mark the beginning of a transformative journey that would redefine his approach to leadership.

The workshop took place in a serene retreat nestled amidst lush greenery, far removed from the hustle and bustle of the corporate world. Jonathan found himself among a diverse group of leaders, all seeking to unlock the secrets of mindful management.

As Dr. Summers took the stage, her presence commanded attention. With warmth and wisdom, she introduced the concept of neurolinguistics and its profound implications for leadership effectiveness. Jonathan listened intently, feeling a sense of recognition stirring within him as Dr. Summers spoke of the power of language to shape perceptions and behaviors.

Through interactive exercises and thought-provoking discussions, Jonathan began to see his own leadership challenges in a new light. He realized that true leadership was not just about making decisions and issuing directives but about connecting with others on a deeper level, understanding their perspectives, and inspiring them to achieve their full potential.

As the workshop drew to a close, Jonathan felt a renewed sense of purpose and clarity. He knew that integrating neurolinguistic principles into his management practices would not be easy, but he was determined to embark on this journey of self-discovery and transformation.

Armed with newfound knowledge and a sense of possibility, Jonathan returned to his company, ready to lead with mindfulness and intentionality. Little did he know, the real work was only just beginning.

Understanding the principles of mindfulness in management

Back in the bustling headquarters of his tech company, Jonathan gathered his management team for a special meeting. As they settled into the conference room, Jonathan's excitement was palpable.

"Thank you all for being here," Jonathan began, his voice filled with conviction. "I recently attended a workshop on mindful management, and I believe the principles I've learned could revolutionize how we lead and operate as a team."

Intrigued, his team leaned in, eager to hear more.

Jonathan delved into the first subpoint: understanding the principles of mindfulness in management. He explained how mindfulness was not just about meditation or relaxation but about being fully present in the moment, cultivating awareness, and fostering a deeper connection with oneself and others.

"As leaders, we're often caught up in the whirlwind of deadlines and deliverables, but true leadership requires us to slow down and truly listen," Jonathan emphasized.

He shared anecdotes from the workshop, illustrating how mindfulness practices had enabled leaders to cultivate empathy, enhance decision-making, and foster a culture of trust and collaboration within their organizations.

As Jonathan spoke, his team began to grasp the profound implications of mindfulness in management. They realized that by embracing mindfulness, they could create a more inclusive and resilient workplace where creativity flourished, and innovation thrived.

Inspired by Jonathan's vision, the management team committed to integrating mindfulness practices into their daily routines. They agreed to start each meeting with a brief mindfulness exercise, setting the tone for open communication and constructive collaboration.

As they adjourned the meeting, Jonathan felt a sense of optimism wash over him. He knew that by embracing mindfulness in their leadership approach, they were not only poised to achieve greater success as a company but also to make a positive impact on the lives of their employees and the communities they served.

The role of Neurolinguistic in Enhancing Mindfulness

With the energy of newfound purpose still coursing through him, Jonathan reconvened his management team for the next phase of their journey: exploring the role of neurolinguistics in enhancing mindfulness.

"Team, our journey towards mindful management continues," Jonathan announced, his voice carrying a tone of determination. "Today, we'll delve into the fascinating world of neurolinguistics and its profound impact on our ability to lead mindfully."

Intrigued, the team leaned in, ready to absorb Jonathan's insights.

Jonathan began by explaining the fundamental principles of neurolinguistics—the study of how language shapes our thoughts, emotions, and behaviors. He emphasized how our choice of words and communication patterns could either enhance or hinder our ability to cultivate mindfulness and connection with others.

"As leaders, our words carry immense power," Jonathan

stressed. "By becoming more aware of how we communicate and understanding the neurological processes at play, we can harness this power to foster deeper connections and create a more mindful workplace culture."

To illustrate his point, Jonathan shared examples of neurolinguistic techniques that leaders could use to enhance mindfulness within their teams. From employing positive language and reframing negative thoughts to practicing active listening and empathy, he demonstrated how small shifts in communication could yield significant results.

As the team absorbed Jonathan's teachings, they began to see the potential for transformation in their own leadership practices. They realized that by adopting neurolinguistic principles, they could cultivate a workplace environment where mindfulness, empathy, and authenticity thrived.

Inspired by Jonathan's guidance, the team committed to incorporating neurolinguistic techniques into their daily interactions. They pledged to approach communication with greater intentionality, recognizing the profound impact their words could have on the well-being and productivity of their colleagues.

As the meeting drew to a close, Jonathan felt a sense of satisfaction knowing that they were on the right path. With mindfulness and neurolinguistics as their guiding lights, they were poised to lead with greater purpose, compassion, and effectiveness than ever before.

Overview of the book's structure and objectives

With a sense of anticipation hanging in the air, Jonathan prepared to unveil the final piece of their journey towards mindful management: an overview of the book's structure and objectives.

"My dear team," Jonathan began, his voice infused with enthusiasm, "as we embark on this transformative journey, it's crucial that we have a roadmap to guide us along the way. That's why I've outlined the structure and objectives of our upcoming book, 'Mindful Management: Harnessing the Power of Neurolinguistics.'"

He paused for effect, allowing the anticipation to build among his eager audience.

"Firstly, the book will be divided into three main sections," Jonathan continued. "The first section will lay the groundwork by exploring the fundamental principles of mindfulness and neurolinguistics, as we've discussed today. This will provide the necessary foundation for us to delve deeper into the practical applications of these concepts in the context of leadership and management."

His team nodded in understanding, fully engaged in the vision Jonathan was laying out before them.

"In the second section," Jonathan continued, "we'll explore a range of topics, from communication and conflict resolution to motivation and emotional intelligence. Each chapter will offer practical insights, real-world examples, and actionable strategies for integrating mindfulness and neurolinguistics into our daily leadership practices."

His team exchanged excited glances, eager to dive into the wealth of knowledge that lay ahead.

"Finally, in the third section," Jonathan concluded, "we'll reflect on our journey and look towards the future, exploring emerging trends, challenges, and opportunities in the realm of mindful management. Our ultimate objective is to equip ourselves with the tools and insights needed to lead with authenticity, compassion, and effectiveness in an ever-evolving business landscape."

As Jonathan outlined the book's structure and objectives, his team felt a sense of clarity and purpose wash over them. They knew that this book would not only serve as a guide for their own personal and professional growth but also as a beacon of inspiration for leaders everywhere who sought to lead with mindfulness and intentionality.

With their path illuminated before them, Jonathan and his team were ready to embark on their journey towards mindful management, armed with the transformative power of neurolinguistics and the unwavering determination to lead with purpose and compassion.

Chapter 2: Foundations of Neurolinguistic

In the quiet sanctuary of a cozy library, Jonathan sat immersed in a sea of books, his brow furrowed in concentration as he delved into the depths of neurolinguistics. Surrounding him were towering shelves filled with volumes on the intricacies of language and the mysteries of the human mind.

As he turned the pages of yet another scholarly work, Jonathan felt a sense of exhilaration wash over him. The foundations of neurolinguistics were revealing themselves to him, like pieces of a puzzle falling into place.

With each word he read, Jonathan gained a deeper understanding of how language shapes our thoughts, emotions, and behaviors. He marveled at the intricate dance between the brain and language, the way neural pathways formed and shifted with every word spoken and heard.

Lost in the world of neurolinguistics, Jonathan felt a sense of wonder at the profound implications of this field of study. He realized that by unraveling the mysteries of language, he could unlock new realms of possibility in his quest for mindful management.

But as Jonathan immersed himself further into the study of neurolinguistics, he encountered challenges and complexities he had never before imagined. The intricacies of the brain's language processing mechanisms, the nuances of linguistic patterns and structures—it was a labyrinth of knowledge, with twists and turns at every corner.

Yet, despite the obstacles, Jonathan was undeterred. He was determined to master the foundations of neurolinguistics, to understand its principles and applications with a clarity and depth that would rival even the most seasoned scholars.

And so, with a steadfast resolve and an insatiable thirst for knowledge, Jonathan delved deeper into the world of neurolinguistics, confident that he was on the brink of a discovery that would revolutionize not only his own leadership practices but the very fabric of the business world itself.

Exploring the basics of Neurolinguistic

Jonathan's journey into the depths of neurolinguistics continued unabated, his thirst for knowledge driving him ever forward. In the dim glow of his study lamp, he poured over textbooks and research papers, eager to unravel the mysteries that lay hidden within the intricate web of language and the brain.

As he delved deeper into the subject, Jonathan found himself captivated by the basics of neurolinguistics. He marveled at the brain's remarkable ability to process language, to decode the symbols and sounds that comprised the fabric of human communication.

With each discovery, Jonathan's understanding grew, like a beacon of light piercing through the darkness of ignorance. He learned about the different regions of the brain involved in language processing, from the Broca's area responsible for speech production to the Wernicke's area responsible for language comprehension.

But it was not just the anatomical structures that fascinated Jonathan—it was the intricate dance between language and cognition, the way in which words shaped our thoughts and perceptions of the world around us.

As he pored over the research, Jonathan began to see the world with new eyes, to recognize the subtle nuances of language that had previously eluded him. He realized that every word we spoke, every phrase we uttered, carried with it a wealth of meaning and significance, shaping our interactions and influencing our behavior in ways both profound and subtle.

With each passing day, Jonathan's passion for neurolinguistics grew, fueled by the promise of unlocking new realms of possibility in the realm of mindful management. He knew that by mastering the basics of neurolinguistics, he could pave the way for a new era of leadership—one grounded in empathy, authenticity, and a deep understanding of the power of words.

And so, with a renewed sense of purpose, Jonathan forged ahead, his mind ablaze with the possibilities that lay ahead. For in the world of neurolinguistics, he had found not just a field of study, but a pathway to transformation—a pathway that would lead him to new heights of leadership and success.

How language shapes perceptions and behaviors

Jonathan's exploration into neurolinguistics delved deeper, leading him to a profound realization: language was not just a tool for communication, but a powerful force that shaped perceptions and behaviors in ways both subtle and profound.

In the quiet solitude of his study, Jonathan poured over the research, his mind racing with newfound insights. He learned how the words we use to describe ourselves and others could influence how we see ourselves and those around us, shaping our identities and relationships in profound ways.

As he delved deeper into the research, Jonathan was struck by the concept of linguistic relativity—the idea that the language we speak influences how we perceive the world. He realized that different languages offered different perspectives on reality, with some cultures having words to describe concepts that were absent in others.

With each revelation, Jonathan's understanding of the power of language deepened. He saw how words could be used to uplift and inspire, to build connections and foster understanding. But he also saw how they could be used to manipulate and deceive, to sow discord and division.

Armed with this newfound knowledge, Jonathan resolved to be mindful of the language he used in his leadership role. He understood that the words he spoke had the power to shape the culture of his organization, to inspire his team to greatness or to sow doubt and mistrust.

And so, with a renewed sense of purpose, Jonathan set out to harness the power of language for positive change. He vowed to lead with integrity and authenticity, to use his words to uplift and empower those around him, and to create a culture of openness, trust, and collaboration within his organization.

As he closed his books and extinguished the study lamp, Jonathan felt a sense of excitement and anticipation. He knew that his journey into neurolinguistics was just beginning, but he was eager to see where it would lead him. For in the power of language, he had found a pathway to transformation—a pathway that would lead him to new heights of leadership and success.

Neurological mechanisms underlying language processing

As Jonathan delved deeper into the neurological mechanisms underlying language processing, he realized the importance of sharing his newfound knowledge with his management team. He arranged for a series of meetings, each held in a different location to inspire creativity and foster a sense of exploration.

The first meeting took place in the company's innovation hub, a sleek, futuristic space filled with cutting-edge technology and vibrant energy. Jonathan and his team gathered around a sleek conference table, surrounded by screens displaying graphs and charts illustrating the brain's intricate neural pathways.

As Jonathan explained the complex interplay between language and the brain, his team listened intently, their eyes alight with curiosity. Together, they explored the fascinating ways in which different regions of the brain processed language, from the auditory cortex responsible for decoding sounds to the frontal lobes involved in higher-order language functions.

As the meeting progressed, the team's excitement grew, fueled by the potential applications of this knowledge in their everyday work. They brainstormed ideas for leveraging neurolinguistics to enhance communication and collaboration within their teams, envisioning a future where every interaction was infused with mindfulness and intentionality.

Buoyed by the success of their first meeting, Jonathan decided to shake things up for the next gathering. He arranged for the team to meet at a tranquil retreat nestled in the heart of nature, far removed from the distractions of the office.

As they gathered around a crackling fire beneath a canopy of stars, Jonathan continued to delve into the mysteries of neurolinguistics. Against the backdrop of rustling leaves and chirping crickets, the team discussed the ways in which language could shape perceptions and behaviors, reflecting on their own experiences and insights.

Inspired by the serenity of their surroundings, the team began to see the world with fresh eyes, recognizing the power of language to influence not only their own thoughts and actions but those of their colleagues and clients as well.

As the meeting drew to a close, Jonathan and his team felt a sense of renewal wash over them. They knew that their journey into neurolinguistics was just beginning, but they were excited to continue exploring the depths of this fascinating field together, armed with the knowledge that they were on the brink of unlocking new realms of possibility in the realm of mindful management.

Chapter 3: Leadership Communication and Influence

In the sleek confines of their company's executive boardroom, Jonathan stood at the head of the table, his gaze steady and his demeanor resolute. Around him, his management team sat poised and attentive, eager to delve into the next chapter of their journey: leadership communication and influence.

"Thank you all for joining me today," Jonathan began, his voice commanding attention. "As leaders, our ability to communicate effectively and influence others is paramount to our success. Today, we'll explore how we can harness the power of neurolinguistics to enhance our communication skills and inspire those around us."

With a sense of anticipation hanging in the air, Jonathan delved into the intricacies of leadership communication, drawing upon his own experiences and insights as well as the latest research in the field of neurolinguistics.

He spoke of the importance of authenticity and clarity in communication, emphasizing the need for leaders to speak

CHAPTER 3: LEADERSHIP COMMUNICATION AND INFLUENCE

with honesty and conviction, and to convey their message in a way that resonated with their audience.

As he spoke, Jonathan's words seemed to ignite a spark within his team, inspiring them to reflect on their own communication styles and the impact they had on those around them.

Together, they explored the power of language to build rapport and trust, to inspire action and drive change. They discussed the importance of active listening and empathy, and how these qualities could help leaders connect with their teams on a deeper level.

But perhaps most importantly, they delved into the concept of influence—the ability to inspire others to embrace a shared vision and work towards a common goal. Jonathan shared examples of leaders who had used neurolinguistic techniques to influence hearts and minds, to galvanize teams and organizations towards greatness.

As the meeting drew to a close, Jonathan and his team felt a sense of empowerment wash over them. They knew that by mastering the principles of leadership communication and influence, they could unlock new levels of success not only for themselves but for their company as a whole.

Armed with this newfound knowledge and inspiration, Jonathan and his team were ready to step boldly into the future, confident in their ability to lead with authenticity, clarity, and influence. For in the world of mindful management, they knew that communication was not just a skill—it was a superpower, capable of transforming lives and shaping the destiny of nations.

Leveraging language patterns for effective leadership

In the heart of their bustling headquarters, Jonathan convened his management team once again, this time with a specific focus on leveraging language patterns for effective leadership. As they gathered in the sleek conference room, anticipation crackled in the air, each member eager to uncover the secrets of persuasive communication.

With a confident stride, Jonathan stepped to the front of the room, a stack of papers clutched in his hand. "Today, we delve into the art of language," he announced, his voice ringing with authority. "Language is more than just words—it's a powerful tool that can shape perceptions, influence decisions, and inspire action."

As he began to outline the various language patterns and techniques that leaders could employ to enhance their effectiveness, Jonathan's passion for the subject was palpable. He spoke of the power of storytelling, of weaving narratives that captured the imagination and stirred the soul. He shared examples of leaders who had used metaphor and analogy to simplify complex concepts and inspire profound insights.

But it wasn't just the content of the message that mattered—it was also the way it was delivered. Jonathan stressed the importance of tone, pacing, and nonverbal cues in effective communication, demonstrating how subtle shifts in language could have a profound impact on how a message was received.

As the meeting progressed, Jonathan encouraged his team to practice using these language patterns in their own communications, offering feedback and guidance along the way. Together, they explored the nuances of persuasion, experimenting with different approaches to see what resonated most with their audience.

As the meeting drew to a close, Jonathan couldn't help but feel a sense of pride in his team. They had embraced the challenge of mastering language patterns for effective leadership with enthusiasm and determination, and he knew that they were well on their way to becoming true masters of the art of communication.

Armed with their newfound knowledge and skills, Jonathan and his team were ready to step confidently into the world, prepared to inspire, influence, and lead with clarity, conviction, and compassion. For in the world of mindful management, they knew that the power of language was not just a tool—it was the key to unlocking limitless possibilities for growth, innovation, and success.

Building rapport and trust through linguistic techniques

In the intimate setting of a cozy coffee shop, Jonathan and his management team gathered for their next discussion, focused on building rapport and trust through linguistic techniques. Surrounded by the comforting aroma of freshly brewed coffee and the gentle hum of conversation, they settled into their seats, ready to explore this crucial aspect of effective leadership.

With a warm smile, Jonathan greeted his team, his eyes twinkling with anticipation. "Today, we embark on a journey into the heart of communication—building rapport and trust," he announced, his voice filled with enthusiasm. "For without trust, leadership is but a hollow shell."

As he spoke, Jonathan delved into the intricacies of rapport-building, emphasizing the importance of establishing genuine connections with others. He shared techniques for mirroring body language and matching vocal tone, demonstrating how these subtle cues could create a sense of harmony and understanding between individuals.

But building rapport was more than just mimicking behavior—it was also about fostering empathy and understanding. Jonathan encouraged his team to listen actively, to seek to understand before seeking to be understood, and to approach every interaction with a genuine desire to connect.

As the discussion unfolded, Jonathan shared personal anecdotes and insights, illustrating how linguistic techniques had helped him forge deep and meaningful relationships with colleagues, clients, and stakeholders. He spoke of the power of authenticity and vulnerability, of being willing to share one's own experiences and emotions in order to build trust and rapport with others.

His team listened intently, nodding in agreement as they absorbed Jonathan's wisdom. They realized that building rapport and trust was not just a skill—it was an art, requiring patience, empathy, and a willingness to step outside of one's comfort zone.

As the meeting drew to a close, Jonathan and his team felt a sense of camaraderie and connection that transcended the boundaries of their professional roles. They knew that by mastering the linguistic techniques of rapport-building, they could create a workplace culture where trust flourished, collaboration thrived, and success was inevitable.

Armed with this newfound understanding, Jonathan and his team left the coffee shop with a renewed sense of purpose and determination. For in the world of mindful management, they knew that trust was the foundation upon which all great achievements were built, and they were committed to nurturing

Influencing others positively using Neurolinguistic strategies

In the vibrant atmosphere of a bustling coworking space, Jonathan and his management team gathered once more, this time to explore the art of influencing others positively using neurolinguistic strategies. Surrounded by the energy of entrepreneurs and innovators, they settled into their seats, ready to uncover the secrets of persuasive communication.

With a gleam of determination in his eyes, Jonathan began to outline the principles of neurolinguistic influence, drawing upon the latest research and insights in the field. He spoke of the power of language to shape beliefs and behaviors, to inspire action and drive change.

"As leaders, it's our responsibility to wield this power wisely," Jonathan declared, his voice ringing with conviction. "We must use our words to uplift and empower those around us, to inspire them to reach their full potential."

With that, Jonathan delved into the nuances of neurolinguistic persuasion, sharing techniques for framing messages in a way that resonated with the values and desires of their audience. He spoke of the importance of using positive language and framing statements in terms of opportunities rather than obstacles, demonstrating how these subtle shifts could make all the difference in how a message was received.

But influencing others positively was not just about what was said—it was also about how it was said. Jonathan encouraged his team to pay attention to their tone of voice, their body language, and their facial expressions, recognizing that these nonverbal cues could have a profound impact on the effectiveness of their communication.

As the discussion unfolded, Jonathan shared examples of leaders who had used neurolinguistic strategies to inspire greatness in others, to motivate teams to achieve extraordinary results, and to foster a culture of innovation and collaboration within their organizations.

His team listened intently, captivated by Jonathan's words and inspired by his vision. They realized that by mastering the principles of neurolinguistic influence, they could become true agents of positive change in the world, using their words to uplift and empower those around them.

As the meeting drew to a close, Jonathan and his team felt a sense of excitement and anticipation. They knew that they had only scratched the surface of what was possible with neurolinguistic persuasion, but they were eager to continue exploring its potential and harnessing its power to create a brighter future for themselves and their organization.

4

Chapter 4: Motivation and Goal Setting

In the tranquil surroundings of a serene retreat nestled amidst rolling hills and towering trees, Jonathan and his management team gathered for their next meeting, focused on the critical topics of motivation and goal setting. Surrounded by the beauty of nature, they found themselves inspired by the promise of growth and transformation that lay ahead.

As they settled into their seats around a rustic wooden table, Jonathan's eyes gleamed with enthusiasm. "Today, we embark on a journey into the heart of motivation and goal setting," he announced, his voice carrying the weight of his conviction. "For without clear goals and unwavering motivation, our dreams remain but distant mirages."

With that, Jonathan delved into the intricacies of motivation, sharing insights gleaned from years of study and experience. He spoke of the importance of intrinsic motivation—the drive that comes from within—and how leaders could foster it in themselves and their teams.

"As leaders, it's our responsibility to inspire greatness in others," Jonathan declared, his words echoing across the tranquil landscape. "We must create an environment where individuals are empowered to pursue their passions and unleash their full potential."

As the discussion unfolded, Jonathan shared strategies for setting meaningful goals and creating a roadmap for success. He emphasized the importance of setting SMART goals—specific, measurable, achievable, relevant, and time-bound—and how these criteria could help individuals and teams stay focused and motivated.

But motivation was not just about setting goals—it was also about cultivating a mindset of resilience and determination. Jonathan encouraged his team to embrace failure as a stepping stone to success, to view setbacks as opportunities for growth, and to approach every challenge with optimism and perseverance.

As the meeting progressed, Jonathan's team found themselves inspired by his words, eager to put his insights into practice in their own lives and work. They realized that by setting clear goals and cultivating unwavering motivation, they could achieve extraordinary results and make a lasting impact on the world around them.

As the sun dipped below the horizon and the meeting drew to a close, Jonathan and his team felt a sense of excitement and anticipation for the journey that lay ahead. They knew that with clarity of purpose and unwavering determination, they could overcome any obstacle and achieve greatness beyond their wildest dreams. And so, with hearts full of hope and minds ablaze with possibility, they set forth into the unknown, ready to conquer new horizons and make their mark on the world.

Utilizing language to motivate teams and individuals

In the heart of their company's vibrant office space, Jonathan and his management team reconvened to delve deeper into the topic of motivation and goal setting, with a specific focus on utilizing language to inspire and motivate teams and individuals. Surrounded by the hum of activity and the buzz of conversation, they gathered around a sleek conference table, ready to uncover the secrets of effective communication.

With a sense of purpose in his voice, Jonathan began to outline the principles of motivational language, drawing upon his own experiences and insights as well as the latest research in the field. He spoke of the power of words to ignite passion, to fuel ambition, and to propel individuals and teams towards greatness.

"As leaders, it's our responsibility to create a culture of motivation and inspiration," Jonathan declared, his voice ringing with conviction. "We must use our words to uplift and empower those around us, to instill a sense of purpose and drive that transcends the daily grind."

With that, Jonathan delved into the nuances of motivational language, sharing techniques for crafting messages that resonated with the values and aspirations of their audience. He spoke of the importance of using positive affirmations and reinforcement, of acknowledging and celebrating the achievements of individuals and teams, and of framing challenges as opportunities for growth and development.

But motivational language was not just about what was said—it was also about how it was said. Jonathan encouraged his team to pay attention to their tone of voice, their body language, and their facial expressions, recognizing that these nonverbal cues could have a profound impact on the effectiveness of their communication.

As the discussion unfolded, Jonathan shared examples of leaders who had used motivational language to inspire greatness in others, to galvanize teams to achieve extraordinary results, and to create a culture of innovation and excellence within their organizations.

His team listened intently, captivated by Jonathan's words and inspired by his vision. They realized that by mastering the principles of motivational language, they could become true catalysts for positive change in the world, using their words to uplift and empower those around them.

As the meeting drew to a close, Jonathan and his team felt a sense of excitement and anticipation. They knew that they had only scratched the surface of what was possible with motivational language, but they were eager to continue exploring its potential and harnessing its power to create a brighter future for themselves and their organization.

Setting SMART goals with a Neurolinguistic approach

In a tranquil meeting room overlooking the city skyline, Jonathan and his management team gathered once more, this time to explore the art of setting SMART goals with a neurolinguistic approach. Surrounded by panoramic views of the bustling city below, they found themselves inspired by the promise of clarity and focus that lay ahead.

With a sense of purpose in his voice, Jonathan began to outline the principles of goal setting, drawing upon the latest research

CHAPTER 4: MOTIVATION AND GOAL SETTING

and insights in neurolinguistics. He spoke of the importance of setting goals that were specific, measurable, achievable, relevant, and time-bound—SMART goals that provided a clear roadmap for success.

"As leaders, it's our responsibility to set the stage for success," Jonathan declared, his voice carrying the weight of his conviction. "We must create a vision for the future that is both ambitious and attainable, and then break it down into smaller, manageable steps that can be achieved over time."

With that, Jonathan delved into the intricacies of SMART goal setting, sharing techniques for crafting goals that resonated with the values and aspirations of their team members. He emphasized the importance of using language that was both clear and compelling, that sparked excitement and enthusiasm in those tasked with achieving them.

But setting SMART goals was not just about what was said—it was also about how it was communicated. Jonathan encouraged his team to paint a vivid picture of success, to use language that evoked emotion and inspiration, and to create a sense of urgency and accountability that propelled individuals and teams towards their objectives.

As the discussion unfolded, Jonathan shared examples of leaders who had used SMART goal setting with a neurolinguistic approach to achieve extraordinary results, to motivate teams to overcome obstacles, and to create a culture of excellence and achievement within their organizations.

His team listened intently, captivated by Jonathan's words and inspired by his vision. They realized that by mastering the principles of SMART goal setting with a neurolinguistic approach, they could become true architects of their own destiny, using their words to chart a course for success and bring their boldest dreams to life.

As the meeting drew to a close, Jonathan and his team felt a sense of excitement and anticipation. They knew that they had only scratched the surface of what was possible with SMART goal setting and neurolinguistics, but they were eager to continue exploring its potential and harnessing its power to create a future that was bright, bold, and full of promise.

Overcoming barriers to motivation through linguistic reframing

In the heart of their company's innovation lab, Jonathan and his management team reconvened once again, this time to explore the topic of overcoming barriers to motivation through linguistic reframing. Surrounded by the hum of creativity and the buzz of innovation, they gathered around a sleek, futuristic table, ready to uncover the secrets of transforming obstacles into opportunities.

With a determined glint in his eye, Jonathan began to outline the principles of linguistic reframing, drawing upon his own experiences and insights as well as the latest research in the field. He spoke of the power of language to shape perceptions, to influence attitudes, and to reframe challenges as opportunities for growth and learning.

"As leaders, it's our responsibility to empower others to overcome adversity," Jonathan declared, his voice resonating with conviction. "We must use our words to inspire resilience, to foster a sense of optimism and possibility, even in the face of the most daunting challenges."

With that, Jonathan delved into the intricacies of linguistic reframing, sharing techniques for shifting perspective and reframing negative situations in a positive light. He emphasized the importance of using language that was both affirming and empowering, that encouraged individuals to see setbacks not as failures but as stepping stones to success.

But linguistic reframing was not just about what was said—it was also about how it was said. Jonathan encouraged his team to infuse their words with empathy and understanding, to acknowledge the emotions and experiences of others, and to offer words of encouragement and support that lifted spirits and renewed hope.

As the discussion unfolded, Jonathan shared examples of leaders who had used linguistic reframing to inspire greatness in others, to motivate teams to overcome seemingly insurmountable obstacles, and to create a culture of resilience and innovation within their organizations.

His team listened intently, captivated by Jonathan's words and inspired by his vision. They realized that by mastering the principles of linguistic reframing, they could become true agents of positive change in the world, using their words to transform adversity into opportunity and to create a future that was bright, bold, and full of promise.

As the meeting drew to a close, Jonathan and his team felt a sense of excitement and anticipation. They knew that they had only scratched the surface of what was possible with linguistic reframing, but they were eager to continue exploring its potential and harnessing its power to overcome barriers to motivation and achieve greatness beyond their wildest dreams.

Chapter 5: Conflict Resolution and Negotiation

In the tranquil setting of a peaceful retreat nestled amidst lush greenery and babbling brooks, Jonathan and his management team gathered for their next meeting, focused on the critical topics of conflict resolution and negotiation. Surrounded by the serenity of nature, they found themselves inspired by the promise of harmony and collaboration that lay ahead.

With a sense of purpose in his voice, Jonathan began to outline the principles of conflict resolution and negotiation, drawing upon his own experiences and insights as well as the latest research in the field. He spoke of the importance of fostering open communication, of seeking common ground, and of approaching conflicts with empathy and understanding.

"As leaders, it's our responsibility to create an environment where conflicts are addressed openly and resolved constructively," Jonathan declared, his voice carrying the weight of his conviction. "We must use our words to facilitate dialogue, to build bridges, and to find win-win solutions that benefit all parties involved."

With that, Jonathan delved into the intricacies of conflict resolution, sharing techniques for de-escalating tensions and finding common ground. He emphasized the importance of active listening and empathy, of seeking to understand before seeking to be understood, and of approaching conflicts with a mindset of collaboration rather than confrontation.

But conflict resolution was not just about finding common ground—it was also about negotiating mutually beneficial outcomes. Jonathan encouraged his team to approach negotiations with confidence and creativity, to explore alternative solutions and to find compromises that satisfied the needs and interests of all parties involved.

As the discussion unfolded, Jonathan shared examples of leaders who had used conflict resolution and negotiation skills to diffuse tense situations, to build trust and goodwill, and to create a culture of cooperation and collaboration within their organizations.

His team listened intently, captivated by Jonathan's words and inspired by his vision. They realized that by mastering the principles of conflict resolution and negotiation, they could become true peacemakers and problem-solvers in the world, using their words to bridge divides and build a future that was harmonious and prosperous for all.

As the meeting drew to a close, Jonathan and his team felt a sense of peace and optimism wash over them. They knew that they had the skills and the knowledge to navigate even the most challenging conflicts and negotiations, and they were eager to put them into practice in their own lives and work. With hearts full of hope and minds ablaze with possibility, they set forth into the world, ready to build a future that was built on collaboration, understanding, and mutual respect.

Managing conflicts using language patterns and communication styles

In the tranquil retreat, surrounded by the rustling of leaves and the gentle flow of water, Jonathan and his management team delved deeper into the intricacies of conflict resolution, this time focusing on managing conflicts using language patterns and communication styles. With a serene determination, they settled into their seats, ready to explore the art of diplomacy and dialogue.

Jonathan's voice resonated with calm authority as he began to outline the principles of managing conflicts through language patterns and communication styles. He spoke of the importance of choosing words carefully, of using language that was both assertive and empathetic, and of adopting communication styles that fostered understanding and collaboration.

"As leaders, it's our responsibility to navigate conflicts with grace and diplomacy," Jonathan declared, his voice carrying the weight of his conviction. "We must use our words to de-escalate tensions, to build trust, and to find common ground that allows for resolution."

With that, Jonathan delved into the nuances of language patterns and communication styles, sharing techniques for diffusing conflicts and fostering productive dialogue. He emphasized the importance of remaining calm and composed, of actively listening to the concerns of all parties involved, and of reframing negative statements into opportunities for constructive discussion.

But managing conflicts was not just about what was said—it

was also about how it was said. Jonathan encouraged his team to adopt communication styles that were both assertive and empathetic, striking a balance between standing their ground and showing understanding towards the perspectives of others.

As the discussion unfolded, Jonathan shared examples of leaders who had used language patterns and communication styles to successfully navigate conflicts, to build bridges between opposing parties, and to create a culture of trust and cooperation within their organizations.

His team listened intently, captivated by Jonathan's words and inspired by his vision. They realized that by mastering the art of managing conflicts through language patterns and communication styles, they could become true peacemakers and problem-solvers in the world, using their words to heal divisions and build bridges between people.

As the meeting drew to a close, Jonathan and his team felt a sense of confidence and optimism wash over them. They knew that they had the skills and the knowledge to navigate even the most challenging conflicts, and they were eager to put them into practice in their own lives and work. With hearts full of hope and minds ablaze with possibility, they set forth into the world, ready to build a future that was built on understanding, empathy, and mutual respect.

Negotiation tactics informed by Neurolinguistic

In the tranquil ambiance of their serene surroundings, Jonathan and his management team continued their exploration into conflict resolution and negotiation, this time focusing on negotiation tactics informed by neurolinguistics. With a sense of purpose in the air, they settled into their seats, ready to uncover the secrets of persuasive communication and strategic negotiation.

Jonathan's voice carried a tone of quiet confidence as he began to delve into the principles of negotiation tactics informed by neurolinguistics. He spoke of the importance of understanding the subconscious triggers that influence decision-making, of using language patterns to build rapport and trust, and of employing strategic techniques to achieve favorable outcomes in negotiations.

"As leaders, it's our responsibility to approach negotiations with skill and finesse," Jonathan declared, his voice resonating with authority. "We must use our words to influence perceptions, to shape outcomes, and to create win-win scenarios that benefit all parties involved."

With that, Jonathan delved into the intricacies of negotiation tactics, sharing techniques for leveraging neurolinguistic principles to achieve desired results. He emphasized the importance of framing proposals in a way that appealed to the values and interests of the other party, of using language patterns to establish rapport and build trust, and of employing subtle cues to influence behavior and decision-making.

But negotiation tactics informed by neurolinguistics were not just about what was said—it was also about how it was said. Jonathan encouraged his team to pay attention to their tone of voice, their body language, and their nonverbal cues, recognizing that these subtle signals could have a powerful impact on the dynamics of a negotiation.

As the discussion unfolded, Jonathan shared examples of leaders who had used negotiation tactics informed by neurolinguistics to achieve remarkable results, to forge strategic alliances, and to create mutually beneficial partnerships within their industries.

His team listened intently, captivated by Jonathan's words and inspired by his vision. They realized that by mastering the principles of negotiation tactics informed by neurolinguistics, they could become true masters of persuasion and influence, using their words to shape the course of events and achieve their most ambitious goals.

As the meeting drew to a close, Jonathan and his team felt a sense of empowerment wash over them. They knew that they had the skills and the knowledge to navigate even the most complex negotiations, and they were eager to put them into practice in their own lives and work. With hearts full of determination and minds ablaze with possibility, they set forth into the world, ready to negotiate their way to success and prosperity.

Turning challenging conversations into Opportunities for resolution

In the midst of their tranquil retreat, Jonathan and his management team delved deeper into the intricacies of conflict resolution and negotiation, focusing now on the art of turning challenging conversations into opportunities for resolution. With a sense of determination in the air, they gathered around the table, ready to explore the transformative power of dialogue and diplomacy.

Jonathan's voice carried a tone of quiet confidence as he began to outline the principles of turning challenging conversations into opportunities for resolution. He spoke of the importance of approaching difficult discussions with empathy and understanding, of seeking common ground even in the face of disagreement, and of using language patterns to foster open communication and build trust.

"As leaders, it's our responsibility to turn conflict into collaboration," Jonathan declared, his voice resonating with conviction. "We must use our words to bridge divides, to find common ground, and to create win-win solutions that benefit all parties involved."

With that, Jonathan delved into the intricacies of transforming challenging conversations into opportunities for resolution, sharing techniques for reframing negative statements, de-escalating tensions, and finding creative solutions to seemingly intractable problems. He emphasized the importance of active listening and empathy, of seeking to understand before seeking to be understood, and of approaching every conversation with a genuine desire to find a mutually satisfactory outcome.

But turning challenging conversations into opportunities for resolution was not just about what was said—it was also about how it was said. Jonathan encouraged his team to adopt communication styles that were both assertive and empathetic, striking a balance between standing their ground and showing understanding towards the perspectives of others.

As the discussion unfolded, Jonathan shared examples of leaders who had used these techniques to successfully navigate challenging conversations, to build trust and goodwill, and to create a culture of openness and collaboration within their organizations.

His team listened intently, captivated by Jonathan's words and inspired by his vision. They realized that by mastering the art of turning challenging conversations into opportunities for resolution, they could become true agents of positive change in the world, using their words to heal divisions and build bridges between people.

As the meeting drew to a close, Jonathan and his team felt a sense of hope and optimism wash over them. They knew that they had the skills and the knowledge to navigate even the most difficult conversations, and they were eager to put them into practice in their own lives and work. With hearts full of compassion and minds ablaze with possibility, they set forth into the world, ready to transform conflict into collaboration and create a future that was built on understanding, empathy, and mutual respect.

Chapter 6: Emotional Intelligence and Self-Awareness

In the serene setting of a tranquil garden, Jonathan and his management team gathered for their next meeting, ready to explore the profound topics of emotional intelligence and self-awareness. Surrounded by the vibrant colors of blooming flowers and the gentle rustling of leaves, they found themselves inspired by the promise of personal growth and introspection that lay ahead.

With a sense of anticipation in the air, Jonathan began to outline the principles of emotional intelligence and self-awareness, drawing upon his own journey of self-discovery and the latest research in the field. He spoke of the importance of understanding and managing one's own emotions, of empathizing with others, and of fostering meaningful connections in both personal and professional settings.

"As leaders, it's our responsibility to cultivate emotional intelligence and self-awareness," Jonathan declared, his voice carrying the weight of his conviction. "We must strive to understand ourselves and others on a deeper level, to navigate the complexities of human emotions with grace and empathy."

With that, Jonathan delved into the intricacies of emotional intelligence and self-awareness, sharing techniques for recognizing and regulating emotions, for developing empathy and compassion, and for building strong relationships based on trust and mutual respect.

He spoke of the importance of self-reflection and introspection, of taking the time to explore one's own thoughts, feelings, and motivations in order to gain a deeper understanding of oneself and others. He emphasized the importance of mindfulness and presence, of being fully engaged in the present moment and open to the experiences and perspectives of those around us.

As the discussion unfolded, Jonathan shared examples of leaders who had cultivated emotional intelligence and self-awareness to become more effective communicators, collaborators, and decision-makers. He spoke of the profound impact that these qualities had on their personal and professional lives, and of the transformative power of self-awareness in creating a more harmonious and fulfilling existence.

His team listened intently, captivated by Jonathan's words and inspired by his vision. They realized that by mastering the principles of emotional intelligence and self-awareness, they could become true leaders in every sense of the word, guiding themselves and others towards greater fulfillment, success, and happiness.

As the meeting drew to a close, Jonathan and his team felt a sense of peace and clarity wash over them. They knew that they had embarked on a journey of self-discovery and growth that would transform not only their professional lives but their personal lives as well. With hearts full of hope and minds open to possibility, they set forth into the world, ready to embrace the challenges and opportunities that lay ahead with courage, compassion, and self-awareness.

Developing emotional intelligence through language awareness

In the serene garden setting, Jonathan and his management team delved deeper into the exploration of emotional intelligence, this time focusing on developing it through language awareness. Surrounded by the soothing sounds of nature, they settled into their seats, ready to uncover the profound connection between language and emotions.

With a calm and steady voice, Jonathan began to outline the principles of developing emotional intelligence through language awareness. He spoke of the power of words to shape our thoughts and feelings, to influence our perceptions and behaviors, and to connect us with others on a deeper level.

"As leaders, it's essential that we become aware of the language we use, both internally and externally," Jonathan declared, his voice resonating with conviction. "By paying attention to our words, we can gain insight into our own emotions and those of others, and cultivate greater empathy, understanding, and connection."

With that, Jonathan delved into the intricacies of language awareness, sharing techniques for recognizing and reframing unhelpful or negative language patterns. He emphasized the importance of using language that was both accurate and empowering, that encouraged self-reflection and growth, and that fostered positive interactions and relationships.

But developing emotional intelligence through language

awareness was not just about what was said—it was also about how it was said. Jonathan encouraged his team to pay attention to their tone of voice, their body language, and their nonverbal cues, recognizing that these subtle signals could reveal a wealth of information about their own emotions and the emotions of others.

As the discussion unfolded, Jonathan shared examples of leaders who had developed emotional intelligence through language awareness to become more effective communicators, collaborators, and leaders. He spoke of the profound impact that this awareness had on their ability to navigate challenges, build strong relationships, and create a culture of trust and respect within their organizations.

His team listened intently, captivated by Jonathan's words and inspired by his vision. They realized that by mastering the principles of developing emotional intelligence through language awareness, they could become true masters of their own emotions and the emotions of others, using their words to foster connection, understanding, and harmony in every aspect of their lives.

As the meeting drew to a close, Jonathan and his team felt a sense of empowerment wash over them. They knew that they had the tools and the knowledge to cultivate greater emotional intelligence and create a more fulfilling and meaningful existence. With hearts full of gratitude and minds open to possibility, they set forth into the world, ready to embrace the journey of self-discovery and growth that lay ahead with courage, compassion, and language awareness.

Recognizing and regulating emotions using linguistic cues

In the tranquil garden sanctuary, Jonathan and his management team ventured deeper into their exploration of emotional intelligence, now honing in on the crucial skill of recognizing and regulating emotions using linguistic cues. Surrounded by the peaceful whispers of nature, they gathered with a newfound sense of curiosity, eager to unlock the secrets of emotional self-awareness.

With a gentle yet firm voice, Jonathan began to unravel the intricacies of recognizing and regulating emotions through linguistic cues. He spoke of the subtle ways in which language revealed our innermost thoughts and feelings, and how paying attention to these cues could empower them to navigate the turbulent seas of emotion with grace and composure.

"As leaders, it's imperative that we learn to recognize and regulate our emotions, not only for our own well-being but for the well-being of those we lead," Jonathan asserted, his words carrying a weight of wisdom. "By understanding the linguistic cues that accompany different emotional states, we can gain insight into our own emotional landscape and effectively manage our responses in any situation."

With that, Jonathan delved into the depths of linguistic cues, sharing techniques for deciphering the hidden messages buried within our words. He emphasized the importance of listening not only to what was said but also to how it was said, noting the subtle shifts in tone, cadence, and choice of words that hinted at underlying emotions.

But recognizing and regulating emotions through linguistic cues was not just about deciphering the language of others—

it was also about mastering the language of self. Jonathan encouraged his team to become attuned to their own internal dialogue, to notice the ways in which their thoughts and words reflected their emotional state, and to cultivate a practice of self-awareness and self-compassion.

As the discussion unfolded, Jonathan shared examples of leaders who had mastered the art of recognizing and regulating emotions through linguistic cues, using their newfound awareness to defuse conflicts, inspire confidence, and foster a culture of trust and collaboration within their organizations.

His team listened intently, captivated by Jonathan's words and inspired by his vision. They realized that by mastering the skill of recognizing and regulating emotions through linguistic cues, they could become true architects of their own emotional landscape, navigating the highs and lows of leadership with poise and resilience.

As the meeting drew to a close, Jonathan and his team felt a sense of empowerment wash over them. They knew that they had the tools and the knowledge to navigate the complexities of human emotion, and they were ready to embrace the journey of emotional self-awareness and mastery that lay ahead with courage, compassion, and linguistic cues.

Cultivating self-awareness for effective management practices

In the tranquil garden setting, Jonathan and his management team delved deeper into their exploration of emotional intelligence, now focusing on the vital practice of cultivating self-awareness for effective management. Surrounded by the serenity of nature, they gathered with a renewed sense of purpose, ready to uncover the profound impact of self-awareness on their leadership journey.

With a calm and resolute voice, Jonathan began to elucidate the principles of cultivating self-awareness for effective management practices. He spoke of the transformative power of introspection and self-reflection, of the importance of understanding one's strengths, weaknesses, and blind spots, and of the profound influence that self-awareness had on every aspect of leadership.

"As leaders, it's essential that we cultivate self-awareness in order to lead authentically and effectively," Jonathan asserted, his words carrying a weight of conviction. "By understanding ourselves on a deeper level, we can better understand and connect with those we lead, and make more informed decisions that align with our values and goals."

With that, Jonathan delved into the intricacies of self-awareness, sharing techniques for cultivating a deeper understanding of oneself and one's motivations. He emphasized the importance of regular self-assessment and feedback, of seeking out diverse perspectives and experiences, and of embracing vulnerability as a pathway to growth and self-discovery.

But cultivating self-awareness for effective management

practices was not just about understanding oneself—it was also about understanding how one's actions and decisions impacted others. Jonathan encouraged his team to pay attention to the ripple effects of their leadership, to consider the perspectives and needs of those they led, and to strive for greater empathy, compassion, and humility in their interactions.

As the discussion unfolded, Jonathan shared examples of leaders who had cultivated self-awareness for effective management practices, using their deep understanding of themselves and others to inspire trust, foster collaboration, and drive meaningful change within their organizations.

His team listened intently, captivated by Jonathan's words and inspired by his vision. They realized that by mastering the practice of cultivating self-awareness, they could become true leaders in every sense of the word, guiding themselves and others towards greater fulfillment, success, and happiness.

As the meeting drew to a close, Jonathan and his team felt a sense of clarity and purpose wash over them. They knew that they had embarked on a journey of self-discovery and growth that would not only transform their leadership practices but also their lives. With hearts full of gratitude and minds open to possibility, they set forth into the world, ready to embrace the challenges and opportunities that lay ahead with courage, compassion, and self-awareness.

7

Chapter 7: Mindful Decision Making

In the serene ambiance of a tranquil garden, Jonathan and his management team gathered for their next meeting, poised to explore the profound topic of mindful decision-making. Surrounded by the gentle rustle of leaves and the sweet scent of blossoms, they settled into their seats with a sense of anticipation, ready to unlock the secrets of clarity and wisdom in their decision-making process.

With a calm and steady voice, Jonathan initiated the discussion on mindful decision-making. He spoke of the importance of approaching decisions with intention, awareness, and an open mind, and of the transformative power of mindfulness in guiding them towards choices that aligned with their values and goals.

"As leaders, our decisions shape the trajectory of our organizations and the lives of those we lead," Jonathan asserted, his words carrying a weight of responsibility. "By cultivating mindfulness in our decision-making process, we can navigate the complexities of leadership with clarity, compassion, and wisdom."

CHAPTER 7: MINDFUL DECISION MAKING

With that, Jonathan delved into the intricacies of mindful decision-making, sharing techniques for cultivating presence, awareness, and discernment in every choice they faced. He emphasized the importance of tuning into their intuition, of quieting the noise of their minds, and of embracing a beginner's mindset that welcomed new perspectives and possibilities.

But mindful decision-making was not just about making the right choice—it was also about making choices that were aligned with their values and aspirations. Jonathan encouraged his team to reflect on their values and priorities, to consider the long-term consequences of their decisions, and to approach every choice with a sense of purpose and integrity.

As the discussion unfolded, Jonathan shared examples of leaders who had embraced mindful decision-making, using their clarity of mind and depth of insight to navigate even the most challenging situations with grace and wisdom. He spoke of the profound impact that mindfulness had on their leadership journey, guiding them towards decisions that fostered growth, innovation, and positive change within their organizations.

His team listened intently, captivated by Jonathan's words and inspired by his vision. They realized that by mastering the practice of mindful decision-making, they could become true stewards of their organizations, guiding them towards a future that was built on clarity, compassion, and wisdom.

As the meeting drew to a close, Jonathan and his team felt a sense of empowerment wash over them. They knew that they had the tools and the knowledge to navigate the complexities of leadership with mindfulness and intention, and they were ready to embrace the journey of mindful decision-making with courage, compassion, and wisdom.

Making informed decisions with a mindful approach

In the serene garden sanctuary, Jonathan and his management team delved deeper into their exploration of mindful decision-making, focusing now on the critical subpoint of making informed decisions with a mindful approach. Surrounded by the tranquility of nature, they gathered with renewed focus, ready to uncover the essence of clarity and insight in their decision-making process.

With a calm yet purposeful demeanor, Jonathan began to elucidate the principles of making informed decisions with a mindful approach. He spoke of the importance of gathering and analyzing relevant information, of considering diverse perspectives and potential outcomes, and of embracing a balanced and discerning mindset in every decision they faced.

"As leaders, it's imperative that we make informed decisions that are grounded in reality and guided by wisdom," Jonathan asserted, his voice carrying a tone of conviction. "By approaching decision-making with mindfulness, we can cut through the noise and complexity, and discern the best course of action for ourselves and our organizations."

With that, Jonathan delved into the intricacies of making informed decisions with a mindful approach, sharing techniques for gathering and synthesizing information, for discerning between fact and opinion, and for navigating uncertainty with courage and clarity.

He emphasized the importance of taking a step back and considering the bigger picture, of weighing the potential risks and rewards of each decision, and of cultivating a sense of curiosity and openness that allowed for new insights and possibilities to emerge.

But making informed decisions with a mindful approach was not just about rational analysis—it was also about tapping into their intuition and inner wisdom. Jonathan encouraged his team to listen to their gut instincts, to trust their inner guidance, and to approach every decision with a sense of presence and awareness that allowed for deeper insight and understanding.

As the discussion unfolded, Jonathan shared examples of leaders who had made informed decisions with a mindful approach, using their clarity of mind and depth of insight to navigate complex challenges and seize opportunities with confidence and grace.

His team listened intently, captivated by Jonathan's words and inspired by his vision. They realized that by mastering the practice of making informed decisions with a mindful approach, they could become true architects of their own destiny, guiding themselves and their organizations towards a future that was grounded in wisdom, insight, and possibility.

As the meeting drew to a close, Jonathan and his team felt a sense of empowerment wash over them. They knew that they had the tools and the knowledge to navigate the complexities of decision-making with mindfulness and discernment, and they were ready to embrace the journey of informed decision-making with courage, clarity, and wisdom.

Analyzing cognitive biases and linguistic influences on decision-making

In the serene garden sanctuary, Jonathan and his management team ventured deeper into their exploration of mindful decision-making, focusing now on the critical subpoint of analyzing cognitive biases and linguistic influences on decision-making. Surrounded by the tranquil beauty of nature, they gathered with heightened curiosity, eager to unravel the mysteries of the mind and language in shaping their choices.

With a calm and deliberate tone, Jonathan initiated the discussion on cognitive biases and linguistic influences on decision-making. He spoke of the subtle ways in which the human mind could be swayed by unconscious biases and linguistic cues, leading to decisions that were flawed or irrational.

"As leaders, it's crucial that we understand the biases and linguistic influences that may cloud our judgment and influence our decisions," Jonathan asserted, his voice carrying a sense of urgency. "By shining a light on these hidden influences, we can cultivate greater awareness and discernment in our decision-making process."

With that, Jonathan delved into the intricacies of cognitive biases, sharing examples of common biases such as confirmation bias, anchoring bias, and availability bias. He emphasized the importance of recognizing these biases in oneself and others, and of actively seeking to mitigate their impact on decision-making through mindfulness and critical thinking.

But understanding cognitive biases was only half of the equation—linguistic influences also played a significant role in shaping decisions. Jonathan encouraged his team to pay attention to the language used in discussions and negotiations, noting how subtle linguistic cues could sway opinions and influence outcomes.

He spoke of the power of framing and priming, where the way a question or statement was phrased could lead to different responses or interpretations. He urged his team to be vigilant in their use of language, ensuring that their words were clear, unbiased, and conducive to rational decision-making.

As the discussion unfolded, Jonathan shared examples of leaders who had fallen prey to cognitive biases and linguistic influences, resulting in costly mistakes and missed opportunities. He emphasized the importance of humility and self-awareness in recognizing these influences and actively working to counteract them in their decision-making process.

His team listened intently, captivated by Jonathan's words and inspired by his vision. They realized that by mastering the art of analyzing cognitive biases and linguistic influences on decision-making, they could become true guardians of rationality and clarity in their leadership roles.

As the meeting drew to a close, Jonathan and his team felt a renewed sense of determination wash over them. They knew that they had the tools and the knowledge to navigate the complexities of decision-making with mindfulness and discernment, and they were ready to embrace the challenge of overcoming cognitive biases and linguistic influences with courage, clarity, and wisdom.

Enhancing decision-making skills through Neurolinguistic techniques

In the tranquil garden sanctuary, Jonathan and his management team delved even deeper into their exploration of mindful decision-making, focusing now on the transformative potential of enhancing decision-making skills through Neurolinguistic techniques. Surrounded by the serene beauty of nature, they gathered with a heightened sense of curiosity and anticipation, eager to uncover the secrets of leveraging Neurolinguistic insights to sharpen their decision-making acumen.

With a calm yet determined demeanor, Jonathan embarked on the discussion of enhancing decision-making skills through Neurolinguistic techniques. He spoke of the powerful interplay between the mind, language, and behavior, and how understanding this dynamic could empower them to make more informed and effective decisions.

"As leaders, it's essential that we harness the power of Neurolinguistic techniques to enhance our decision-making skills," Jonathan asserted, his voice resonating with conviction. "By tapping into the underlying mechanisms of language and cognition, we can unlock new insights, perspectives, and strategies that elevate our decision-making to new heights."

With that, Jonathan delved into the intricacies of Neurolinguistic techniques, sharing examples of how they could be applied to decision-making processes. He spoke of techniques such as reframing, which involved shifting the perspective or context of a decision to uncover new possibilities and solutions. He also discussed the importance of anchoring, where they could use language and imagery to create mental associations that guided their decision-making in a desired direction.

CHAPTER 7: MINDFUL DECISION MAKING

But enhancing decision-making skills through Neurolinguistic techniques was not just about applying these techniques externally—it was also about cultivating a deeper understanding of oneself and one's cognitive processes. Jonathan encouraged his team to explore their own thought patterns, beliefs, and biases, and to use Neurolinguistic techniques to challenge and reframe them as needed.

As the discussion unfolded, Jonathan shared examples of leaders who had successfully applied Neurolinguistic techniques to enhance their decision-making skills, using their newfound insights to navigate complex challenges and seize opportunities with confidence and clarity.

His team listened intently, captivated by Jonathan's words and inspired by his vision. They realized that by mastering the art of Neurolinguistic techniques, they could become true masters of their own minds and destinies, guiding themselves and their organizations towards greater success and fulfillment.

As the meeting drew to a close, Jonathan and his team felt a sense of excitement and possibility wash over them. They knew that they had embarked on a journey of discovery and growth that would not only transform their decision-making skills but also their lives. With hearts full of determination and minds open to possibility, they set forth into the world, ready to embrace the power of Neurolinguistic techniques with courage, clarity, and wisdom.

Chapter 8: Performance Feedback and Coaching

In the tranquil setting of a secluded garden, Jonathan and his management team gathered once more, this time to explore the vital topic of performance feedback and coaching. Surrounded by the serene beauty of nature, they settled into their seats with a sense of purpose, ready to delve into the intricacies of guiding and developing their team members towards greater success.

With a calm and authoritative presence, Jonathan initiated the discussion on performance feedback and coaching. He spoke of the importance of providing constructive feedback that empowered team members to grow and improve, and of the transformative impact that effective coaching could have on individual and organizational performance.

"As leaders, it's our responsibility to support and develop our team members, helping them to reach their full potential and achieve their goals," Jonathan asserted, his voice carrying the weight of his conviction. "By offering meaningful feedback and guidance, we can foster a culture of continuous learning and improvement that drives success and innovation."

With that, Jonathan delved into the intricacies of performance feedback and coaching, sharing techniques for delivering feedback in a way that was constructive, specific, and actionable. He emphasized the importance of creating a safe and supportive environment where team members felt valued and respected, and where feedback was seen as an opportunity for growth rather than criticism.

But performance feedback and coaching were not just about providing feedback—it was also about guiding and supporting team members on their journey towards success. Jonathan encouraged his team to take a proactive approach to coaching, actively seeking out opportunities to mentor and develop their team members, and to provide the support and resources needed to help them excel.

As the discussion unfolded, Jonathan shared examples of leaders who had embraced performance feedback and coaching as a cornerstone of their leadership philosophy, using their guidance and support to unlock the full potential of their teams and drive exceptional results.

His team listened intently, captivated by Jonathan's words and inspired by his vision. They realized that by mastering the art of performance feedback and coaching, they could become true catalysts for growth and success within their organizations, guiding their teams towards excellence with wisdom, empathy, and compassion.

As the meeting drew to a close, Jonathan and his team felt a sense of excitement and possibility wash over them. They knew that they had embarked on a journey of transformation and empowerment that would not only elevate their team's performance but also enrich their lives. With hearts full of determination and minds open to possibility, they set forth into the world, ready to embrace the power of performance feedback and coaching with courage, clarity, and conviction.

Providing constructive feedback using language precision

In the serene garden retreat, Jonathan and his management team delved deeper into their exploration of performance feedback and coaching, now focusing on the critical subpoint of providing constructive feedback using language precision. Surrounded by the tranquility of nature, they gathered with renewed focus, ready to uncover the nuances of communication that could drive meaningful growth and development within their team.

With a calm and measured tone, Jonathan embarked on the discussion of providing constructive feedback using language precision. He spoke of the importance of clarity, specificity, and empathy in delivering feedback that empowered team members to excel and grow.

"As leaders, it's crucial that we communicate with precision and care when providing feedback to our team members," Jonathan asserted, his voice carrying a tone of sincerity. "By using language that is clear, specific, and empathetic, we can create an environment where feedback is seen as a valuable opportunity for learning and improvement."

With that, Jonathan delved into the intricacies of language precision in feedback, sharing techniques for crafting messages that were both honest and constructive. He emphasized the importance of focusing on behaviors rather than personalities, of providing specific examples and actionable suggestions, and of acknowledging the efforts and strengths of team members even in the midst of criticism.

But providing constructive feedback using language precision was not just about what was said—it was also about how it was said. Jonathan encouraged his team to pay attention to their tone of voice, their body language, and their choice of words, recognizing that these subtle cues could have a profound impact on how feedback was received.

As the discussion unfolded, Jonathan shared examples of leaders who had mastered the art of providing constructive feedback using language precision, using their words to inspire growth, resilience, and accountability within their teams.

His team listened intently, captivated by Jonathan's words and inspired by his vision. They realized that by mastering the skill of language precision in feedback, they could become true agents of positive change within their organization, guiding their team members towards greater success and fulfillment with wisdom, empathy, and clarity.

As the meeting drew to a close, Jonathan and his team felt a sense of empowerment wash over them. They knew that they had the tools and the knowledge to communicate effectively and compassionately, and they were ready to embrace the challenge of providing constructive feedback with courage, integrity, and precision.

Coaching for success with neurolinguistic coaching models

In the tranquil garden sanctuary, Jonathan and his management team delved even deeper into their exploration of performance feedback and coaching, now honing in on the transformative power of coaching for success with Neurolinguistic coaching models. Surrounded by the soothing ambiance of nature, they gathered with a sense of purpose, ready to unlock the full potential of their coaching interactions.

With a composed yet enthusiastic demeanor, Jonathan embarked on the discussion of coaching for success with Neurolinguistic coaching models. He spoke of the profound impact that understanding the interplay between language, behavior, and cognition could have on coaching effectiveness.

"As leaders, our role as coaches is to inspire and empower our team members to reach their full potential," Jonathan asserted, his voice resonating with passion. "By leveraging Neurolinguistic coaching models, we can unlock new insights and strategies that enable meaningful growth and transformation."

With that, Jonathan delved into the intricacies of Neurolinguistic coaching models, sharing techniques for aligning communication styles with individual preferences, for eliciting deeper insights through powerful questioning, and for facilitating positive change through language and behavior patterns.

He emphasized the importance of building rapport and trust with team members, of creating a safe and supportive space for exploration and discovery, and of tailoring coaching approaches to meet the unique needs and goals of each individual.

But coaching for success with Neurolinguistic coaching models was not just about techniques—it was also about mindset and intention. Jonathan encouraged his team to approach coaching with a sense of curiosity, openness, and empathy, recognizing that true transformation arose from a deep understanding of the individual and their unique experiences.

As the discussion unfolded, Jonathan shared examples of leaders who had embraced Neurolinguistic coaching models to drive remarkable results within their teams. He spoke of the profound impact that these approaches had on empowering individuals to overcome challenges, capitalize on opportunities, and achieve their highest aspirations.

His team listened intently, captivated by Jonathan's words and inspired by his vision. They realized that by mastering the art of coaching for success with Neurolinguistic coaching models, they could become true catalysts for growth and change within their organization, guiding their team members towards greatness with wisdom, empathy, and skill.

As the meeting drew to a close, Jonathan and his team felt a renewed sense of purpose and possibility wash over them. They knew that they had embarked on a journey of empowerment and transformation that would not only elevate their coaching effectiveness but also enrich their lives. With hearts full of determination and minds open to possibility, they set forth into the world, ready to embrace the power of Neurolinguistic coaching models with courage, compassion, and conviction.

Creating a supportive environment for professional growth through communication

In the tranquil garden oasis, Jonathan and his management team ventured deeper into their exploration of performance feedback and coaching, focusing now on the pivotal subpoint of creating a supportive environment for professional growth through communication. Surrounded by the serene beauty of nature, they gathered with a renewed sense of purpose, ready to cultivate an atmosphere where every team member could thrive and flourish.

With a composed and empathetic demeanor, Jonathan initiated the discussion on creating a supportive environment for professional growth through communication. He spoke of the profound impact that open, honest, and empathetic communication could have on fostering trust, collaboration, and innovation within the team.

"As leaders, it's our responsibility to create an environment where every team member feels valued, respected, and empowered to grow and succeed," Jonathan asserted, his voice carrying a tone of sincerity. "By fostering open and supportive communication, we can create a culture of learning and development that drives individual and organizational excellence."

With that, Jonathan delved into the intricacies of communication that supported professional growth, sharing techniques for creating a safe and inclusive space for dialogue, for providing encouragement and constructive feedback, and for celebrating successes and learning from failures.

He emphasized the importance of active listening, of seeking to understand before seeking to be understood, and of fostering a culture where diverse perspectives were welcomed and respected.

But creating a supportive environment for professional growth through communication was not just about what was said—it was also about how it was said. Jonathan encouraged his team to be mindful of their tone, body language, and nonverbal cues, recognizing that these subtle signals could profoundly impact the way their messages were received.

As the discussion unfolded, Jonathan shared examples of leaders who had successfully created a supportive environment for professional growth through communication, using their words and actions to inspire trust, collaboration, and resilience within their teams.

His team listened intently, captivated by Jonathan's words and inspired by his vision. They realized that by mastering the art of communication that supported professional growth, they could create a workplace where every team member could reach their full potential and contribute their unique talents and perspectives to the collective success of the organization.

As the meeting drew to a close, Jonathan and his team felt a sense of optimism and possibility wash over them. They knew that they had embarked on a journey of empowerment and transformation that would not only elevate their team's performance but also enrich their lives. With hearts full of determination and minds open to possibility, they set forth into the world, ready to cultivate a culture of growth and excellence through communication with courage, compassion, and conviction.

Chapter 9: Team Dynamics and Collaboration

In a secluded garden retreat, Jonathan and his management team gathered to delve into the intricate dynamics of teamwork and collaboration. Surrounded by the lush greenery and tranquil sounds of nature, they settled into their seats, ready to explore the power of synergy and collective effort in achieving shared goals.

With a commanding yet approachable presence, Jonathan began to expound upon the essence of team dynamics and collaboration. He spoke of the interdependence of team members, the strength found in diversity, and the transformative potential of working together towards a common purpose.

"As leaders, we must recognize that our success is intertwined with the success of our team," Jonathan declared, his voice resonating with authority. "By fostering a culture of collaboration and cooperation, we can harness the collective genius of our team members to overcome challenges and achieve remarkable results."

With that, Jonathan delved into the intricacies of team

dynamics and collaboration, sharing insights into building cohesive teams, fostering trust and psychological safety, and leveraging the unique strengths of each team member to drive innovation and excellence.

He emphasized the importance of clear communication, mutual respect, and shared accountability in fostering a collaborative environment where ideas could flow freely, and everyone felt valued and supported.

But team dynamics and collaboration were not just about working together—it was also about embracing conflict, learning from differences, and growing stronger as a result. Jonathan encouraged his team to see challenges as opportunities for growth, to approach disagreements with curiosity and openness, and to embrace diversity as a source of strength and creativity.

As the discussion unfolded, Jonathan shared examples of teams that had achieved extraordinary success through collaboration, citing their ability to leverage the diverse skills, perspectives, and experiences of their members to innovate, problem-solve, and achieve ambitious goals.

His team listened intently, captivated by Jonathan's words and inspired by his vision. They realized that by mastering the art of team dynamics and collaboration, they could unlock the full potential of their team, driving performance and innovation to new heights.

As the meeting drew to a close, Jonathan and his team felt a sense of unity and purpose wash over them. They knew that they had embarked on a journey of collaboration and synergy that would not only elevate their team's performance but also foster a sense of belonging and fulfillment among its members. With hearts full of determination and minds open to possibility, they set forth into the world, ready to embrace the power of teamwork with courage, compassion, and conviction.

Fostering collaboration through linguistic alignment

In the serene garden setting, Jonathan and his management team delved deeper into their exploration of team dynamics and collaboration, now focusing on the critical subpoint of fostering collaboration through linguistic alignment. Surrounded by the calming presence of nature, they gathered with heightened awareness, ready to uncover the profound impact of language on the dynamics of teamwork.

With a poised and insightful demeanor, Jonathan initiated the discussion on fostering collaboration through linguistic alignment. He spoke of the power of language to shape perceptions, build rapport, and create a shared sense of purpose among team members.

"As leaders, we must recognize that the language we use has the power to either unite or divide our team," Jonathan asserted, his voice carrying a sense of urgency. "By fostering linguistic alignment, we can create a culture where every voice is heard, every perspective is valued, and every idea is welcomed with open arms."

With that, Jonathan delved into the intricacies of linguistic alignment, sharing techniques for using language to build connections, foster empathy, and inspire collective action. He emphasized the importance of using inclusive and affirming language, of seeking common ground and shared understanding, and of fostering a culture of appreciation and respect in all communication.

But fostering collaboration through linguistic alignment was not just about the words themselves—it was also about the intention behind them. Jonathan encouraged his team to communicate with authenticity and transparency, to speak from the heart and listen with empathy, and to strive for clarity and coherence in their messages.

As the discussion unfolded, Jonathan shared examples of teams that had achieved remarkable success through linguistic alignment, citing their ability to communicate effectively, resolve conflicts constructively, and collaborate seamlessly towards common goals.

His team listened intently, captivated by Jonathan's words and inspired by his vision. They realized that by mastering the art of linguistic alignment, they could create a culture where trust flourished, creativity thrived, and collaboration soared to new heights.

As the meeting drew to a close, Jonathan and his team felt a sense of unity and purpose wash over them. They knew that they had embarked on a journey of collaboration and synergy that would not only elevate their team's performance but also strengthen their bonds and deepen their connections. With hearts full of determination and minds open to possibility, they set forth into the world, ready to harness the power of linguistic alignment with courage, compassion, and conviction.

Building high-performing teams with effective communication strategies

In the tranquil garden sanctuary, Jonathan and his management team ventured further into their exploration of team dynamics and collaboration, now focusing on the essential subpoint of building high-performing teams with effective communication strategies. Surrounded by the serene beauty of nature, they gathered with a heightened sense of purpose, ready to uncover the secrets of fostering synergy and excellence through communication.

With a commanding yet empathetic presence, Jonathan initiated the discussion on building high-performing teams with effective communication strategies. He spoke of the pivotal role that communication played in cultivating trust, promoting transparency, and fostering cohesion within a team.

"As leaders, it's imperative that we employ effective communication strategies to build teams that are greater than the sum of their parts," Jonathan declared, his voice resonating with authority. "By fostering clear, open, and empathetic communication, we can create an environment where every team member feels valued, heard, and empowered to contribute their best."

With that, Jonathan delved into the intricacies of effective communication strategies for building high-performing teams. He shared techniques for fostering open dialogue, promoting active listening, and resolving conflicts constructively. He emphasized the importance of setting clear expectations, providing regular feedback, and celebrating successes as a team.

But building high-performing teams with effective communication strategies was not just about the words spoken—it was also about the quality of relationships forged and the culture cultivated within the team. Jonathan encouraged his team to nurture a culture of trust and psychological safety, where team members felt comfortable expressing their ideas, sharing their concerns, and taking calculated risks.

As the discussion unfolded, Jonathan shared examples of teams that had achieved extraordinary success through effective communication strategies, citing their ability to foster collaboration, innovation, and resilience in the face of challenges.

His team listened intently, captivated by Jonathan's words and inspired by his vision. They realized that by mastering the art of effective communication, they could create a culture where every team member felt empowered to contribute their unique talents and perspectives to the collective success of the team.

As the meeting drew to a close, Jonathan and his team felt a sense of unity and purpose wash over them. They knew that they had embarked on a journey of collaboration and synergy that would not only elevate their team's performance but also enrich their lives. With hearts full of determination and minds open to possibility, they set forth into the world, ready to build high-performing teams with effective communication strategies with courage, compassion, and conviction.

Resolving Conflicts and enhancing synergy within teams using Neurolinguistics

In the serene garden sanctuary, Jonathan and his management team delved even deeper into their exploration of team dynamics and collaboration, now focusing on the critical subpoint of resolving conflicts and enhancing synergy within teams using Neurolinguistics. Surrounded by the tranquility of nature, they gathered with a heightened sense of determination, ready to uncover innovative approaches to fostering harmony and cooperation among team members.

With a composed and insightful demeanor, Jonathan initiated the discussion on resolving conflicts and enhancing synergy within teams using Neurolinguistics. He spoke of the profound impact that understanding the neural mechanisms of language and communication could have on transforming conflicts into opportunities for growth and collaboration.

"As leaders, it's essential that we leverage the insights of Neurolinguistics to resolve conflicts and enhance synergy within our teams," Jonathan asserted, his voice carrying a tone of conviction. "By understanding how language shapes perceptions and behaviors, we can facilitate open dialogue, foster mutual understanding, and build stronger, more cohesive teams."

With that, Jonathan delved into the intricacies of Neurolinguistics in conflict resolution and synergy enhancement, sharing techniques for reframing perspectives, eliciting empathy, and finding common ground through language and communication. He emphasized the importance of active listening, of acknowledging and validating emotions, and of approaching conflicts with curiosity and openness.

But resolving conflicts and enhancing synergy within teams using Neurolinguistics was not just about applying techniques—it was also about cultivating a mindset of empathy, respect, and collaboration. Jonathan encouraged his team to see conflicts as opportunities for learning and growth, to approach them with a spirit of curiosity and openness, and to prioritize understanding and connection over winning or being right.

As the discussion unfolded, Jonathan shared examples of teams that had successfully resolved conflicts and enhanced synergy through Neurolinguistic approaches, citing their ability to transform misunderstandings into opportunities for deeper connection and collaboration.

His team listened intently, captivated by Jonathan's words and inspired by his vision. They realized that by mastering the principles of Neurolinguistics, they could become true architects of harmony and cooperation within their teams, fostering an environment where every member felt valued, respected, and empowered to contribute their best.

As the meeting drew to a close, Jonathan and his team felt a sense of optimism and possibility wash over them. They knew that they had embarked on a journey of transformation and empowerment that would not only elevate their team's performance but also strengthen their bonds and deepen their connections. With hearts full of determination and minds open to possibility, they set forth into the world, ready to resolve conflicts and enhance synergy within their teams using Neurolinguistics with courage, compassion, and conviction.

10

Chapter 10: Change Management and Adaptability

In the midst of the garden's tranquility, Jonathan and his management team gathered once more, this time to explore the dynamic realm of change management and adaptability. Surrounded by the gentle rustle of leaves and the sweet scent of flowers, they settled into their seats with a sense of anticipation, prepared to confront the challenges and opportunities that change inevitably brings.

With a calm yet resolute demeanor, Jonathan initiated the discussion on change management and adaptability. He spoke of the inevitability of change in today's fast-paced world, and the critical importance of embracing it with courage, flexibility, and resilience.

"As leaders, we must recognize that change is not only inevitable but also necessary for growth and progress," Jonathan declared, his voice carrying a tone of conviction. "By fostering adaptability and resilience within ourselves and our teams, we can navigate change with grace and emerge stronger and more resilient than ever before."

CHAPTER 10: CHANGE MANAGEMENT AND ADAPTABILITY

With that, Jonathan delved into the intricacies of change management and adaptability, sharing insights into the psychology of change, the stages of transition, and the strategies for leading teams through periods of uncertainty and transformation. He emphasized the importance of fostering a growth mindset, of embracing uncertainty as an opportunity for learning and growth, and of leading with empathy and compassion during times of change.

But change management and adaptability were not just about navigating external challenges—it was also about fostering a culture of innovation, creativity, and continuous improvement within the team. Jonathan encouraged his team to embrace change as a catalyst for growth, to challenge the status quo, and to seek out new opportunities for learning and development.

As the discussion unfolded, Jonathan shared examples of leaders who had successfully navigated change and led their teams to new heights of success and achievement. He spoke of their ability to inspire confidence, foster collaboration, and drive innovation in the face of adversity.

His team listened intently, captivated by Jonathan's words and inspired by his vision. They realized that by mastering the art of change management and adaptability, they could transform challenges into opportunities and emerge stronger and more resilient than ever before.

As the meeting drew to a close, Jonathan and his team felt a sense of empowerment wash over them. They knew that they had embarked on a journey of growth and transformation that would not only elevate their team's performance but also enrich their lives. With hearts full of determination and minds open to possibility, they set forth into the world, ready to embrace change with courage, resilience, and optimism.

Managing change using language to alleviate resistance

In the boardroom, Jonathan and his management team delved deeper into their exploration of managing change using language to alleviate resistance. With a backdrop of sleek, modern furnishings, they gathered around the polished table, ready to confront the complexities of guiding their organization through times of transition.

Jonathan, his voice steady and resolute, addressed the team, "Change is inevitable, but it's how we navigate it that defines our success. Language is our most powerful tool in managing change, as it has the ability to ease resistance and inspire confidence in our vision."

He delved into the nuances of language, sharing strategies for crafting messages that addressed concerns, acknowledged fears, and inspired hope. He emphasized the importance of transparency, empathy, and clarity in communication, noting that by addressing resistance head-on and fostering understanding, they could create a culture where change was embraced rather than feared.

As the discussion unfolded, Jonathan and his team brainstormed ways to tailor their communication to different stakeholders, recognizing that each individual had their own unique perspective and concerns. They explored techniques for framing change as an opportunity for growth, for highlighting the benefits and opportunities it presented, and for actively involving team members in the process of change.

With each idea shared, the atmosphere in the room shifted from apprehension to excitement. They realized that by harnessing the power of language to alleviate resistance, they could transform challenges into opportunities and lead their organization to new heights of success.

As the meeting drew to a close, Jonathan and his team felt a renewed sense of purpose and determination. They knew that they had the tools and the knowledge to guide their organization through change with confidence and grace. With hearts full of courage and minds open to possibility, they set forth into the future, ready to embrace change as a catalyst for growth and transformation.

Facilitating organizational transitions with neurolingustic tools

In the sleek conference room, Jonathan and his management team ventured further into their exploration of change management, now focusing on the pivotal subpoint of facilitating organizational transitions with Neurolinguistic tools. Surrounded by the hum of technology and the glow of screens, they gathered with a sense of determination, ready to unlock the potential of Neurolinguistic techniques in guiding their organization through periods of transformation.

Jonathan, his demeanor composed yet determined, addressed the team, "In times of change, our ability to navigate transitions effectively can make all the difference. Neurolinguistic tools offer us unique insights into the human mind, allowing us to facilitate transitions with empathy, clarity, and effectiveness."

He delved into the intricacies of Neurolinguistic tools, sharing techniques for understanding and influencing the subconscious mind, for reframing perspectives, and for creating powerful mental associations that guided behavior and decision-making. He emphasized the importance of aligning communication with the neurology of change, using language and imagery to evoke positive emotions, spark inspiration, and foster resilience in the face of uncertainty.

As the discussion unfolded, Jonathan and his team brainstormed ways to integrate Neurolinguistic techniques into their change management strategy. They explored techniques for anchoring positive emotions to the vision of change, for using metaphor and storytelling to communicate complex ideas, and for tapping into the power of visualization to inspire action and commitment.

With each idea shared, the energy in the room crackled with excitement. They realized that by harnessing the power of Neurolinguistic tools, they could create a culture where change was embraced as an opportunity for growth and innovation, rather than feared as a threat to stability and security.

As the meeting drew to a close, Jonathan and his team felt a sense of empowerment wash over them. They knew that they had the tools and the knowledge to guide their organization through transitions with confidence and clarity. With hearts full of courage and minds open to possibility, they set forth into the future, ready to embrace change as a catalyst for transformation and success.

Cultivating adaptability and resilience in the face of change

In the high-tech conference room, Jonathan and his management team embarked on a crucial discussion, focusing on cultivating adaptability and resilience in the face of change. Surrounded by cutting-edge technology and sleek furnishings, they gathered with a shared determination, ready to confront the challenges of an ever-evolving business landscape.

CHAPTER 10: CHANGE MANAGEMENT AND ADAPTABILITY

Jonathan, his voice steady and unwavering, addressed the team, "Adaptability and resilience are the cornerstones of success in today's dynamic world. As leaders, it's our responsibility to foster these qualities within ourselves and our teams, enabling us to thrive in the face of uncertainty and change."

He delved into the essence of adaptability and resilience, sharing insights into the mindset and behaviors that fostered these qualities. He emphasized the importance of embracing change as an opportunity for growth, of maintaining a positive outlook in the face of adversity, and of cultivating a sense of flexibility and openness to new possibilities.

As the discussion unfolded, Jonathan and his team brainstormed strategies for fostering adaptability and resilience within their organization. They explored techniques for promoting a growth mindset, for encouraging experimentation and innovation, and for providing support and resources to help team members navigate transitions with confidence and grace.

With each idea shared, the energy in the room palpably shifted from apprehension to determination. They realized that by cultivating adaptability and resilience, they could not only survive in the face of change but also thrive, emerging stronger and more resilient than ever before.

As the meeting drew to a close, Jonathan and his team felt a renewed sense of purpose and determination. They knew that they had the tools and the knowledge to navigate the uncertainties of the future with courage and resilience. With hearts full of optimism and minds open to possibility, they set forth into the world, ready to embrace change as a catalyst for growth and transformation.

Chapter 11: Creativity and Innovation

In a room filled with vibrant colors, Jonathan and his management team gathered to explore the exhilarating realm of creativity and innovation. Surrounded by art pieces and inspirational quotes, they settled into their seats with a sense of anticipation, ready to unleash their creative potential and drive innovation within their organization.

With a contagious enthusiasm, Jonathan initiated the discussion on creativity and innovation. "Innovation is the lifeblood of progress, and creativity is its spark," he declared, his voice brimming with excitement. "As leaders, it's our duty to cultivate a culture where creativity flourishes, and innovation thrives."

He delved into the essence of creativity and innovation, sharing insights into the power of imagination, curiosity, and experimentation. He emphasized the importance of fostering an environment where ideas were welcomed, risks were encouraged, and failure was seen as a stepping stone to success.

As the discussion unfolded, Jonathan and his team brainstormed strategies for fostering creativity and driving innovation within their organization. They explored techniques for sparking creativity, such as brainstorming sessions, design thinking workshops, and cross-functional collaborations. They also discussed the importance of creating a supportive environment where team members felt empowered to take risks, challenge the status quo, and pursue bold ideas.

With each idea shared, the energy in the room soared to new heights. They realized that by embracing creativity and innovation, they could unlock new possibilities, solve complex problems, and drive meaningful change within their organization and beyond.

As the meeting drew to a close, Jonathan and his team felt a sense of excitement and possibility wash over them. They knew that they had embarked on a journey of discovery and exploration that would not only elevate their organization's performance but also inspire and transform their lives. With hearts full of creativity and minds open to innovation, they set forth into the world, ready to unleash their creative potential and drive innovation with courage, passion, and vision.

Stimulating creativity through linguistic techniques

In the room pulsating with creative energy, Jonathan and his management team delved deeper into their exploration of creativity and innovation, now focusing on the essential subpoint of stimulating creativity through linguistic techniques. Surrounded by colorful artwork and inspirational quotes, they gathered with a renewed sense of curiosity, ready to uncover the power of language in igniting their creative sparks.

With a fervent passion, Jonathan initiated the discussion on stimulating creativity through linguistic techniques. "Language has the power to ignite imagination, spark inspiration, and breathe life into our ideas," he proclaimed, his voice resonating with enthusiasm. "As leaders, it's our responsibility to harness the magic of words to fuel creativity and drive innovation."

He delved into the intricacies of linguistic techniques for stimulating creativity, sharing insights into the art of storytelling, metaphor, and wordplay. He emphasized the importance of using vivid imagery, evocative language, and playful expression to ignite the imagination and inspire fresh perspectives.

As the discussion unfolded, Jonathan and his team brainstormed ways to integrate linguistic techniques into their creative process. They explored techniques for crafting compelling narratives, using metaphor and analogy to unlock new insights, and leveraging the power of language to challenge assumptions and spark breakthrough ideas.

With each idea shared, the room buzzed with excitement. They realized that by embracing linguistic techniques, they could transform their communication into a powerful tool for creativity and innovation, unlocking new possibilities and driving meaningful change within their organization.

As the meeting drew to a close, Jonathan and his team felt a surge of creativity and inspiration wash over them. They knew that they had unlocked a new dimension of possibility, where language was not just a means of communication but a catalyst for transformation and growth. With hearts full of creativity and minds open to possibility, they set forth into the world, ready to unleash their creative potential and drive innovation with courage, passion, and imagination.

CHAPTER 11: CREATIVITY AND INNOVATION

Overcoming mental blocks and fostering innovation with language

In the midst of their creative sanctuary, Jonathan and his management team delved even deeper into their exploration of creativity and innovation, focusing now on the crucial subpoint of overcoming mental blocks and fostering innovation with language. Surrounded by the vibrant hues of their artistic haven, they gathered with a collective determination, ready to unravel the mysteries of the creative process.

With an unwavering resolve, Jonathan addressed the team, "Mental blocks are the silent barriers that hinder our creativity and stifle innovation. Language, however, can be a powerful tool to break through these barriers and unleash our creative potential."

He delved into the nuances of overcoming mental blocks, sharing insights into the power of reframing, positive self-talk, and creative visualization. He emphasized the importance of using language to challenge limiting beliefs, reframe obstacles as opportunities, and cultivate a mindset of resilience and possibility.

As the discussion unfolded, Jonathan and his team brainstormed strategies for overcoming mental blocks and fostering innovation with language. They explored techniques for cultivating a growth mindset, such as affirmations, visualization exercises, and reframing negative thoughts into positive affirmations.

With each idea shared, the energy in the room surged. They realized that by harnessing the power of language, they could transform their inner dialogue, break free from self-imposed limitations, and tap into their limitless creative potential.

As the meeting drew to a close, Jonathan and his team felt a newfound sense of liberation and possibility. They knew that they had the tools and the knowledge to overcome mental blocks and foster innovation with language. With hearts full of courage and minds open to possibility, they set forth into the world, ready to unleash their creativity and drive innovation with unwavering determination and boundless imagination.

Creating a culture of creativity within organizations through mindful management

In the vibrant, art-adorned room, Jonathan and his management team ventured further into their exploration of creativity and innovation, honing in on the transformative subpoint of creating a culture of creativity within organizations through mindful management. Surrounded by the dynamic colors and inspirational ambiance, they gathered with a collective sense of purpose, poised to unravel the secrets of fostering a culture where creativity thrived.

With a calm yet impassioned tone, Jonathan addressed the team, "A culture of creativity is not just a luxury—it's a necessity for organizations to thrive in today's ever-evolving landscape. As mindful leaders, it's our responsibility to cultivate an environment where creativity is nurtured, celebrated, and embraced."

He delved into the essence of creating a culture of creativity, sharing insights into the role of mindful management in fostering innovation. He emphasized the importance of leading by example, creating space for experimentation, and encouraging diversity of thought and perspective.

As the discussion unfolded, Jonathan and his team brainstormed strategies for cultivating a culture of creativity within their organization. They explored techniques for promoting autonomy and ownership, fostering a sense of psychological safety, and providing opportunities for learning and growth.

With each idea shared, the room buzzed with excitement. They realized that by embracing mindful management practices, they could create a culture where creativity flourished, innovation thrived, and every team member felt empowered to contribute their unique talents and perspectives.

As the meeting drew to a close, Jonathan and his team felt a sense of optimism and possibility wash over them. They knew that they had embarked on a journey of transformation, where creativity was not just encouraged but celebrated as the lifeblood of their organization. With hearts full of courage and minds open to possibility, they set forth into the world, ready to cultivate a culture of creativity through mindful management with unwavering dedication and boundless enthusiasm.

12

Chapter 12: Cultural Sensitivity and Diversity

In a room adorned with artifacts representing diverse cultures, Jonathan and his management team gathered to delve into the enriching topic of cultural sensitivity and diversity. Surrounded by the tapestries of global heritage, they settled into their seats with a profound sense of respect, ready to explore the intricate tapestry of human experience that defined their organization's diverse workforce.

With a gentle yet commanding presence, Jonathan initiated the discussion on cultural sensitivity and diversity. "Our organization is a mosaic of cultures, each one contributing to the richness of our collective identity," he remarked, his voice resonating with reverence. "As leaders, it's our responsibility to honor and celebrate this diversity, fostering an environment where every voice is heard, valued, and respected."

He delved into the essence of cultural sensitivity and diversity, sharing insights into the importance of empathy, inclusion, and understanding. He emphasized the need for leaders to embrace cultural humility, to recognize their own biases, and to commit to lifelong learning and growth in their journey towards cultural competence.

As the discussion unfolded, Jonathan and his team exchanged perspectives and experiences, each one offering a unique lens through which to view the complexities of diversity. They explored strategies for promoting cultural sensitivity, such as cross-cultural training, inclusive language practices, and fostering open dialogue.

With each idea shared, the room reverberated with the harmonious melody of unity in diversity. They realized that by embracing cultural sensitivity and diversity, they could create a workplace where every individual felt valued, respected, and empowered to bring their whole selves to work.

As the meeting drew to a close, Jonathan and his team felt a deep sense of gratitude and appreciation for the diverse tapestry of humanity that defined their organization. They knew that they had embarked on a journey of understanding and inclusion, where differences were celebrated as strengths and unity was forged through mutual respect and empathy. With hearts full of compassion and minds open to diversity, they set forth into the world, ready to champion cultural sensitivity and diversity with unwavering commitment and profound respect.

Navigating cultural differences with linguistic sensitivity

In the midst of their cultural haven, Jonathan and his management team delved deeper into their exploration of cultural sensitivity and diversity, now focusing on the vital subpoint of navigating cultural differences with linguistic sensitivity. Surrounded by the symbols of global heritage, they gathered with a heightened awareness, ready to unravel the complexities of communication across cultural boundaries.

With a thoughtful and empathetic demeanor, Jonathan addressed the team, "Language is not just a means of communication; it's a reflection of culture, identity, and values. As mindful leaders, it's our duty to navigate cultural differences with sensitivity and respect, using language as a bridge to connect rather than divide."

He delved into the intricacies of linguistic sensitivity in navigating cultural differences, sharing insights into the power of language to shape perceptions, convey meaning, and build rapport across cultural divides. He emphasized the importance of understanding cultural nuances, adapting communication styles, and practicing active listening to foster genuine understanding and connection.

As the discussion unfolded, Jonathan and his team exchanged perspectives and experiences, each one offering valuable insights into the challenges and opportunities of cross-cultural communication. They explored strategies for navigating cultural differences with linguistic sensitivity, such as using inclusive language, avoiding cultural stereotypes, and seeking clarification when faced with ambiguity.

With each idea shared, the room resonated with a sense of mutual respect and appreciation for the diverse perspectives that enriched their collective experience. They realized that by embracing linguistic sensitivity, they could create a workplace where cultural differences were not barriers but bridges to deeper understanding and collaboration.

As the meeting drew to a close, Jonathan and his team felt a profound sense of unity and purpose. They knew that they had embarked on a journey of cultural sensitivity and diversity, where language served as a powerful tool for building bridges across divides and fostering a culture of inclusion and belonging. With hearts full of empathy and minds open to diversity, they set forth into the world, ready to navigate cultural differences with linguistic sensitivity and forge connections that transcended borders and boundaries.

Communicating in inclusively to promote diversity and belonging

In the sanctuary of cultural understanding, Jonathan and his management team continued their exploration of cultural sensitivity and diversity, now focusing on the indispensable subpoint of communicating inclusively to promote diversity and belonging. Surrounded by the symbols of global heritage, they gathered with a shared commitment to fostering an environment where every voice was heard, valued, and respected.

With a compassionate yet determined tone, Jonathan addressed the team, "Inclusive communication is the cornerstone of building a culture of diversity and belonging. As mindful leaders, it's our responsibility to ensure that every individual feels seen, heard, and valued, regardless of their background or identity."

He delved into the essence of inclusive communication, sharing insights into the power of language to create a sense of belonging, foster empathy, and promote diversity. He emphasized the importance of using inclusive language, actively listening to diverse perspectives, and amplifying marginalized voices to create a culture where everyone felt welcome and accepted.

As the discussion unfolded, Jonathan and his team exchanged ideas and experiences, each one offering a unique perspective on the importance of inclusive communication in promoting diversity and belonging. They explored strategies for communicating inclusively, such as using gender-neutral language, avoiding assumptions based on stereotypes, and creating spaces for open dialogue and constructive feedback.

With each idea shared, the room hummed with a sense of solidarity and unity. They realized that by embracing inclusive communication, they could create a workplace where every individual felt empowered to bring their authentic selves to work, where diversity was celebrated as a strength, and where belonging was not just a concept but a lived experience.

As the meeting drew to a close, Jonathan and his team felt a profound sense of pride and purpose. They knew that they had embarked on a journey of inclusivity and belonging, where every word spoken and every action taken had the power to shape a culture of diversity and acceptance. With hearts full of compassion and minds open to diversity, they set forth into the world, ready to communicate inclusively and promote diversity and belonging with unwavering dedication and profound respect.

Leveraging language to bridge cultural divides and foster collaboration

In the midst of their culturally rich sanctuary, Jonathan and his management team continued their exploration of cultural sensitivity and diversity, now honing in on the pivotal subpoint of leveraging language to bridge cultural divides and foster collaboration. Surrounded by artifacts representing the diverse tapestry of humanity, they gathered with a shared determination to harness the power of language as a force for unity and collaboration.

With a serene yet resolute demeanor, Jonathan addressed the team, "Language has the power to transcend borders and bridges, connecting hearts and minds across cultural divides. As mindful leaders, it's our duty to leverage language as a tool for fostering collaboration and unity, embracing the richness of diversity as a source of strength."

He delved into the intricacies of leveraging language to bridge cultural divides, sharing insights into the art of communication that transcended linguistic and cultural barriers. He emphasized the importance of fostering empathy, curiosity, and openness in our interactions, seeking to understand and appreciate the perspectives of others.

As the discussion unfolded, Jonathan and his team exchanged ideas and experiences, each one offering a unique perspective on the role of language in fostering collaboration across cultures. They explored strategies for leveraging language to bridge cultural divides, such as promoting active listening, using inclusive language, and finding common ground through shared values and aspirations.

With each idea shared, the room buzzed with a sense of possibility and connection. They realized that by embracing language as a tool for collaboration, they could create a workplace where diversity was celebrated as a source of innovation and creativity, and where collaboration flourished across cultural boundaries.

As the meeting drew to a close, Jonathan and his team felt a profound sense of unity and purpose. They knew that they had embarked on a journey of cultural sensitivity and diversity, where language served as a powerful tool for building bridges and fostering collaboration. With hearts full of empathy and minds open to diversity, they set forth into the world, ready to leverage language to bridge cultural divides and create a more inclusive and interconnected future.

13

Chapter 13: Stress Management and Well-being

In a serene room adorned with calming colors and soft lighting, Jonathan and his management team gathered to explore the crucial topic of stress management and well-being. Surrounded by the soothing ambiance, they settled into their seats with a collective sigh of relief, ready to delve into the intricacies of nurturing their mental and emotional health.

With a gentle yet determined demeanor, Jonathan addressed the team, "In the fast-paced world of business, stress can often feel like an unavoidable part of life. However, as mindful leaders, it's our responsibility to prioritize our well-being and cultivate strategies for managing stress effectively."

He delved into the essence of stress management and well-being, sharing insights into the impact of stress on our mental, emotional, and physical health. He emphasized the importance of self-care, resilience, and mindfulness in navigating the challenges of leadership and maintaining a healthy work-life balance.

As the discussion unfolded, Jonathan and his team exchanged

experiences and strategies for managing stress and promoting well-being in their lives. They explored techniques such as meditation, exercise, and time management to help alleviate stress and foster resilience.

With each idea shared, the room filled with a sense of calm and determination. They realized that by prioritizing their well-being, they could not only improve their own quality of life but also enhance their effectiveness as leaders and create a more positive and supportive workplace culture.

As the meeting drew to a close, Jonathan and his team felt a renewed sense of energy and purpose. They knew that they had embarked on a journey of self-discovery and personal growth, where stress was not a burden to bear but an opportunity to cultivate resilience and well-being. With hearts full of determination and minds open to possibility, they set forth into the world, ready to prioritize their well-being and lead with clarity, compassion, and resilience.

Managing stress through mindful language practices

In the tranquil setting of their meeting room, Jonathan and his management team delved deeper into their exploration of stress management and well-being, now focusing on the crucial subpoint of managing stress through mindful language practices. Surrounded by the serene ambiance, they gathered with a shared intention to discover how the power of language could be harnessed to alleviate stress and promote mental resilience.

With a calm yet determined tone, Jonathan addressed the team, "Language is not only a means of communication but also a powerful tool for shaping our thoughts and emotions.

As mindful leaders, it's essential that we harness the power of language to cultivate a positive mindset and manage stress effectively."

He delved into the intricacies of mindful language practices for stress management, sharing insights into the ways in which our words and internal dialogue can either exacerbate or alleviate stress. He emphasized the importance of practicing self-compassion, reframing negative thoughts, and cultivating a sense of gratitude and optimism through mindful language.

As the discussion unfolded, Jonathan and his team exchanged experiences and strategies for integrating mindful language practices into their daily lives. They explored techniques such as positive affirmations, compassionate self-talk, and reframing challenging situations in a more constructive light.

With each idea shared, the room filled with a sense of empowerment and possibility. They realized that by harnessing the power of language to cultivate mindfulness and resilience, they could navigate the inevitable challenges of leadership with greater ease and grace.

As the meeting drew to a close, Jonathan and his team felt a renewed sense of clarity and determination. They knew that they had discovered a powerful tool for managing stress and promoting well-being in their lives. With hearts full of gratitude and minds open to possibility, they set forth into the world, ready to embrace mindful language practices as a pathway to greater resilience and inner peace.

Promoting employee well-being with linguistic support

In the serene atmosphere of their meeting room, Jonathan and his management team delved even deeper into their exploration of stress management and well-being, now focusing on the vital subpoint of promoting employee well-being with linguistic support. Surrounded by the calming ambiance, they gathered with a shared commitment to fostering a workplace culture where the mental and emotional health of every team member was valued and supported.

With a compassionate yet resolute tone, Jonathan addressed the team, "As leaders, it's our responsibility to create an environment where our employees feel seen, heard, and supported in their well-being journey. Language plays a crucial role in this, as the words we use can either uplift and empower or contribute to feelings of stress and anxiety."

He delved into the importance of linguistic support in promoting employee well-being, sharing insights into the ways in which language can be used to provide encouragement, validation, and empathy. He emphasized the need for leaders to cultivate a culture of open communication, where team members felt comfortable expressing their concerns and seeking support when needed.

As the discussion unfolded, Jonathan and his team exchanged ideas and strategies for promoting employee well-being through linguistic support. They explored techniques such as active listening, providing constructive feedback with empathy, and using language to acknowledge and validate the experiences of others.

With each idea shared, the room filled with a sense of compassion and solidarity. They realized that by prioritizing linguistic support for employee well-being, they could create a workplace culture where every team member felt valued, supported, and empowered to thrive.

As the meeting drew to a close, Jonathan and his team felt a profound sense of purpose and commitment. They knew that they had embarked on a journey of transformation, where language served as a powerful tool for promoting employee well-being and fostering a culture of compassion and support. With hearts full of empathy and minds open to possibility, they set forth into the world, ready to uplift and empower their team members with the transformative power of words.

Creating a culture of work-life balance through mindful management approaches

In the tranquil sanctuary of their meeting room, Jonathan and his management team delved even deeper into their exploration of stress management and well-being, now focusing on the indispensable subpoint of creating a culture of work-life balance through mindful management approaches. Surrounded by the soothing ambiance, they gathered with a shared determination to foster an environment where their team members could thrive both personally and professionally.

With a calm yet resolute demeanor, Jonathan addressed the team, "Work-life balance is essential for the well-being and productivity of our team members. As mindful leaders, it's our responsibility to create a culture where work and life harmonize, allowing our team members to lead fulfilling lives both inside and outside the workplace."

He delved into the essence of work-life balance, sharing insights into the importance of setting boundaries, prioritizing self-care, and fostering flexibility in work arrangements. He emphasized the need for leaders to lead by example, modeling healthy work-life integration and encouraging their team members to prioritize their well-being.

As the discussion unfolded, Jonathan and his team exchanged ideas and strategies for creating a culture of work-life balance through mindful management approaches. They explored techniques such as setting realistic expectations, promoting time management skills, and providing resources for self-care and stress management.

With each idea shared, the room filled with a sense of empowerment and possibility. They realized that by prioritizing work-life balance, they could create a workplace where team members felt valued, supported, and empowered to bring their whole selves to work.

As the meeting drew to a close, Jonathan and his team felt a renewed sense of purpose and commitment. They knew that they had embarked on a journey of transformation, where work and life could coexist in harmony, allowing their team members to thrive both personally and professionally. With hearts full of compassion and minds open to possibility, they set forth into the world, ready to create a culture of work-life balance through mindful management approaches and lead by example with unwavering dedication and care.

14

Chapter 14: Ethical Leadership and Integrity

In a room adorned with symbols of ethical values and integrity, Jonathan and his management team gathered to explore the fundamental principles of ethical leadership. Surrounded by reminders of integrity and honesty, they settled into their seats with a shared commitment to uphold the highest standards of moral conduct in their leadership roles.

With a dignified yet approachable demeanor, Jonathan addressed the team, "Ethical leadership is the cornerstone of trust, respect, and integrity within our organization. As leaders, it's our duty to demonstrate unwavering commitment to ethical principles and inspire those around us to do the same."

He delved into the essence of ethical leadership, sharing insights into the importance of honesty, fairness, and transparency in all aspects of decision-making and behavior. He emphasized the need for leaders to lead by example, embodying the values they espoused and holding themselves accountable to the highest ethical standards.

As the discussion unfolded, Jonathan and his team exchanged

ideas and experiences, each one reflecting on their own ethical dilemmas and the importance of navigating them with integrity and conviction. They explored strategies for promoting ethical leadership, such as fostering a culture of open communication, providing ethical training and education, and creating mechanisms for reporting unethical behavior.

With each idea shared, the room resonated with a sense of moral clarity and purpose. They realized that by prioritizing ethical leadership, they could create a workplace where trust and integrity were the foundation of every interaction and decision.

As the meeting drew to a close, Jonathan and his team felt a profound sense of responsibility and honor. They knew that they had embarked on a journey of ethical leadership, where integrity and honesty were not just ideals to strive for but guiding principles to live by. With hearts full of conviction and minds steadfast in their commitment to ethical conduct, they set forth into the world, ready to lead with integrity and inspire others to do the same.

Leading with integrity through language alignment with values

In the sanctum of ethical leadership, Jonathan and his management team delved deeper into their exploration, now focusing on the vital subpoint of leading with integrity through language alignment with values. Surrounded by the aura of ethical consciousness, they gathered with a shared commitment to ensure that every word spoken reflected the core values of honesty, respect, and integrity.

With a steadfast yet empathetic tone, Jonathan addressed the team, "Our language is a reflection of our values and beliefs. As leaders, it's imperative that we align our words with our ethical principles, using language as a tool to inspire trust, foster respect, and uphold integrity in all that we do."

He delved into the intricacies of leading with integrity through language alignment with values, sharing insights into the power of communication to shape organizational culture and influence behavior. He emphasized the need for leaders to be mindful of their language, ensuring that their words were consistent with the ethical standards they espoused and inspiring others to follow suit.

As the discussion unfolded, Jonathan and his team exchanged ideas and strategies for aligning language with values in their leadership practices. They explored techniques such as using inclusive and respectful language, communicating transparently and authentically, and reinforcing ethical values through storytelling and messaging.

With each idea shared, the room resonated with a sense of conviction and purpose. They realized that by leading with integrity through language alignment with values, they could create a culture where ethical behavior was not just expected but celebrated as a hallmark of leadership excellence.

As the meeting drew to a close, Jonathan and his team felt a renewed sense of commitment to their ethical principles. They knew that they had the power to influence positive change through their words and actions, and they were determined to lead with integrity, both in speech and in deed. With hearts full of resolve and minds steadfast in their dedication to ethical conduct, they set forth into the world, ready to inspire others to follow their example and uphold the highest standards of integrity in all aspects of their lives.

Ethical decision-making using neurolinguistic principles

In the solemn chamber of ethical deliberation, Jonathan and his management team ventured further into their exploration, now focusing on the profound subpoint of ethical decision-making using neurolinguistic principles. Surrounded by the weight of their ethical responsibilities, they gathered with a shared commitment to navigate moral complexities with clarity, integrity, and empathy.

With a contemplative yet determined tone, Jonathan addressed the team, "Ethical decision-making requires not only a deep understanding of our values but also an awareness of the cognitive and linguistic processes that shape our perceptions and judgments. As leaders, it's crucial that we leverage neurolinguistic principles to ensure that our decisions are not only ethical but also grounded in empathy and compassion."

He delved into the intricacies of ethical decision-making using neurolinguistic principles, sharing insights into the ways in which language and cognition interact to influence our moral reasoning. He emphasized the importance of self-awareness, emotional regulation, and perspective-taking in navigating ethical dilemmas with integrity and clarity.

As the discussion unfolded, Jonathan and his team exchanged ideas and strategies for applying neurolinguistic principles to ethical decision-making. They explored techniques such as reframing ethical dilemmas, considering multiple perspectives, and using empathetic language to communicate their decisions with transparency and compassion.

With each idea shared, the room resonated with a sense of introspection and empathy. They realized that by integrating neurolinguistic principles into their ethical decision-making processes, they could foster a culture where ethical behavior was not just a matter of compliance but a reflection of their commitment to empathy, fairness, and integrity.

As the meeting drew to a close, Jonathan and his team felt a profound sense of empowerment and clarity. They knew that they had the tools and the wisdom to navigate ethical dilemmas with integrity and compassion, guided by the principles of neurolinguistics. With hearts full of resolve and minds open to possibility, they set forth into the world, ready to lead with ethical conviction and inspire others to do the same.

Building trust and credibility as an ethical leader

In the chamber of ethical deliberation, Jonathan and his management team delved deeper into their exploration, now focusing on the critical subpoint of building trust and credibility as an ethical leader. Surrounded by the weight of their ethical responsibilities, they gathered with a shared commitment to embody integrity, transparency, and authenticity in all their actions and interactions.

With a firm yet compassionate tone, Jonathan addressed the team, "Trust is the foundation of effective leadership, and credibility is earned through consistent demonstration of ethical behavior. As leaders, it's imperative that we cultivate trust and credibility by aligning our words with our actions and upholding the highest standards of integrity in everything we do."

He delved into the intricacies of building trust and credibility as an ethical leader, sharing insights into the importance of transparency, accountability, and authenticity in earning the trust of others. He emphasized the need for leaders to lead by example, demonstrating integrity and ethical conduct in every decision and interaction.

As the discussion unfolded, Jonathan and his team exchanged ideas and strategies for building trust and credibility as ethical leaders. They explored techniques such as leading with transparency, admitting mistakes and taking responsibility for their actions, and fostering open communication and collaboration.

With each idea shared, the room resonated with a sense of solidarity and determination. They realized that by embodying the principles of ethical leadership, they could inspire trust and credibility in their team members, fostering a culture of integrity and accountability.

As the meeting drew to a close, Jonathan and his team felt a renewed sense of purpose and commitment. They knew that they had the power to build trust and credibility as ethical leaders, and they were determined to lead with integrity, transparency, and authenticity in all their endeavors. With hearts full of conviction and minds steadfast in their dedication to ethical conduct, they set forth into the world, ready to inspire trust and credibility and lead by example with unwavering commitment and integrity.

15

Chapter 15: Future Trends and Applications

In a room pulsating with the energy of innovation and possibility, Jonathan and his management team gathered to explore the dynamic landscape of future trends and applications. Surrounded by the hum of anticipation, they settled into their seats with a shared excitement for the opportunities that lay ahead.

With a visionary gleam in his eye, Jonathan addressed the team, "The future is unfolding before us, ripe with potential and promise. As leaders, it's our duty to embrace emerging trends and leverage cutting-edge applications to propel our organization forward into new realms of success."

He delved into the essence of future trends and applications, sharing insights into the transformative technologies and paradigm shifts that were shaping the business landscape. From artificial intelligence to blockchain, from remote work to augmented reality, he painted a vivid picture of the possibilities that awaited those who dared to innovate and adapt.

As the discussion unfolded, Jonathan and his team exchanged

ideas and perspectives, each one contributing their unique insights into the trends and applications that were poised to revolutionize their industry. They explored the implications of emerging technologies, the opportunities for innovation, and the challenges of navigating an ever-changing landscape.

With each idea shared, the room buzzed with excitement and anticipation. They realized that by embracing future trends and applications, they could position their organization at the forefront of innovation, driving growth, and success in the years to come.

As the meeting drew to a close, Jonathan and his team felt a sense of exhilaration and purpose. They knew that they were standing on the brink of a new era, where the possibilities were limited only by their imagination and determination. With hearts full of ambition and minds open to possibility, they set forth into the future, ready to embrace the challenges and opportunities that lay ahead with unwavering optimism and determination.

Exploring emerging trends in neurolingustics and management

In the midst of their visionary gathering, Jonathan and his management team delved deeper into their exploration, now focusing on the captivating subpoint of exploring emerging trends in neurolinguistics and management. Surrounded by the electrifying energy of innovation, they gathered with a shared curiosity to unravel the potential of this burgeoning field.

With a spark of excitement in his eyes, Jonathan addressed the team, "Neurolinguistics is evolving rapidly, offering profound insights into the human mind and behavior. As leaders, it's crucial that we stay at the forefront of these emerging trends, harnessing the power of neurolinguistics to enhance our management practices and drive organizational success."

He delved into the intricacies of emerging trends in neurolinguistics and management, sharing insights into groundbreaking research and innovative applications that were reshaping the way leaders understood and engaged with their teams. From neuroleadership to neurocoaching, from brain-based learning to cognitive enhancement techniques, he painted a vivid picture of the transformative potential of neurolinguistics in the realm of management.

As the discussion unfolded, Jonathan and his team exchanged ideas and perspectives, each one eager to explore the implications of these emerging trends for their organization. They discussed the opportunities for enhancing communication, decision-making, and leadership effectiveness through neurolinguistic insights, as well as the challenges of integrating these cutting-edge practices into their existing management frameworks.

With each idea shared, the room crackled with intellectual curiosity and enthusiasm. They realized that by embracing emerging trends in neurolinguistics and management, they could unlock new levels of performance, innovation, and employee engagement within their organization.

As the meeting drew to a close, Jonathan and his team felt a sense of exhilaration and possibility. They knew that they were embarking on a journey of discovery and transformation, where the boundaries of what was possible were constantly being expanded by the latest advancements in neurolinguistics. With hearts full of excitement and minds open to exploration, they set forth into the future, ready to embrace the challenges and opportunities that lay ahead with unwavering curiosity and determination.

Applications of neurolinguistic approaches in future management practices

In the midst of their visionary gathering, Jonathan and his management team delved deeper into their exploration, now focusing on the captivating subpoint of applications of neurolinguistic approaches in future management practices. Surrounded by the electrifying energy of innovation, they gathered with a shared curiosity to unlock the potential of this groundbreaking fusion.

With a spark of excitement in his eyes, Jonathan addressed the team, "Neurolinguistic approaches offer us a profound understanding of how language shapes perception, behavior, and communication. As leaders, it's imperative that we explore the applications of these insights in shaping the future of management practices, driving organizational success, and fostering employee well-being."

He delved into the intricacies of neurolinguistic approaches in management, sharing insights into the transformative potential of language-based interventions to enhance leadership effectiveness, team dynamics, and organizational culture. From neuroleadership coaching to language-based performance optimization techniques, he painted a vivid picture of the myriad ways in which neurolinguistics could revolutionize the way leaders engage with their teams and drive performance.

As the discussion unfolded, Jonathan and his team exchanged ideas and perspectives, each one eager to explore the practical applications of neurolinguistic approaches in their management practices. They discussed the opportunities for leveraging language to enhance employee motivation, foster psychological safety, and promote collaboration, as well as the challenges of integrating these innovative techniques into their existing leadership frameworks.

With each idea shared, the room crackled with intellectual curiosity and excitement. They realized that by embracing neurolinguistic approaches in their management practices, they could unlock new levels of performance, engagement, and well-being within their organization, propelling them towards a future of sustained success and innovation.

As the meeting drew to a close, Jonathan and his team felt a sense of inspiration and possibility. They knew that they were embarking on a journey of transformation, where the intersection of neurolinguistics and management held the key to unlocking the full potential of their organization and its people. With hearts full of anticipation and minds open to exploration, they set forth into the future, ready to embrace the opportunities that lay ahead with unwavering determination and enthusiasm.

Challenges and opportunities for Integrating neurolinguistics into organizational strategies

In the chamber pulsating with anticipation, Jonathan and his management team delved deeper into their exploration, now focusing on the compelling subpoint of challenges and opportunities for integrating neurolinguistics into organizational strategies. Surrounded by the electrifying energy of innovation, they gathered with a shared determination to navigate the complexities of this transformative endeavor.

With a thoughtful expression, Jonathan addressed the team, "Integrating neurolinguistics into our organizational strategies presents both immense opportunities and significant challenges. As leaders, it's essential that we understand and address these factors to harness the full potential of this powerful discipline."

He delved into the intricacies of integrating neurolinguistics into organizational strategies, sharing insights into the opportunities for enhancing leadership effectiveness, improving communication, and fostering employee engagement through language-based interventions. From neuroleadership development programs to linguistic-based performance evaluations, he painted a comprehensive picture of the potential benefits of integrating neurolinguistics into organizational practices.

However, Jonathan also acknowledged the challenges that lay ahead. He discussed the need for leaders to overcome resistance to change, navigate cultural barriers, and address ethical considerations when implementing neurolinguistic approaches. He emphasized the importance of fostering a culture of openness, experimentation, and continuous learning to overcome these challenges and drive successful integration.

As the discussion unfolded, Jonathan and his team exchanged ideas and perspectives, each one grappling with the complexities and possibilities of integrating neurolinguistics into their organizational strategies. They discussed the need for leadership buy-in, stakeholder engagement, and strategic alignment to ensure the successful implementation of neurolinguistic interventions.

With each idea shared, the room crackled with intellectual curiosity and determination. They realized that by embracing the challenges and opportunities of integrating neurolinguistics into organizational strategies, they could unlock new levels of performance, innovation, and employee engagement within their organization.

As the meeting drew to a close, Jonathan and his team felt a sense of clarity and purpose. They knew that they were embarking on a transformative journey, where the intersection of neurolinguistics and organizational strategy held the key to unlocking the full potential of their organization and its people. With hearts full of determination and minds open to possibility, they set forth into the future, ready to embrace the challenges and opportunities that lay ahead with unwavering commitment and enthusiasm.

About the Author

Goodson Mumba is a multifaceted individual known for his diverse expertise and prolific contributions across various fields. As an infopreneur, thought leader, and spiritual leader, he has inspired countless individuals through his insightful teachings and impactful writings. Mumba is also an accomplished author, with several notable works to his name, including "Understanding Corporate Worship," "The Years I Spent in a Week," "Management By Harmony," "The CEO's Diary," "Change to Change" and "Creative Thinking for results" His literary works span topics ranging from business management to personal development and spirituality, reflecting his broad range of interests and insights.

With a Master of Business Leadership (MBL) and a Bachelor of Arts in Theology (BTh), Mumba brings a unique blend of business acumen and spiritual wisdom to his work. His educational background is further enriched by a Group Diploma in Management Studies, providing him with a solid foundation in organizational dynamics and leadership principles. Additionally, Mumba holds diplomas in Education Psychology,

Leadership and Management Styles, Organizational Behaviour, Financial Accounting, Economic Growth and Development, and Project Management, showcasing his commitment to continuous learning and professional development.

Mumba's expertise extends beyond traditional academic disciplines, encompassing areas such as Neuro-Linguistic Programming (NLP) and Positive Psychology. His diverse skill set is complemented by a range of certifications, including Creative Problem Solving and Decision Making, Life Coaching Fundamentals and Techniques, Professional Life Coaching, and Performance Management System Design. These certifications reflect Mumba's dedication to equipping himself with the tools and knowledge necessary to empower others and drive positive change.

As an author, Mumba's writings reflect his deep understanding of human nature, organizational dynamics, and spiritual principles. His works offer practical insights, actionable strategies, and inspirational guidance for individuals seeking personal growth, professional success, and spiritual fulfillment. Mumba's holistic approach to life and leadership resonates with readers worldwide, making him a respected figure in both the business and spiritual communities.

Overall, Goodson Mumba's diverse background, extensive knowledge, and profound insights make him a sought-after speaker, mentor, and author. His commitment to excellence, lifelong learning, and service to others continues to inspire individuals to unlock their full potential and lead lives of purpose and significance.

Goodson Mumba is renowned for initiating the concept of Management by Harmony, revolutionizing traditional management practices with a focus on balanced and holistic approaches. He has authored two influential books on this subject: "Introduction to Management by Harmony" and its sequel, "Management by Harmony."

Mumba's work has significantly impacted the field, offering innovative strategies for fostering organizational harmony and efficiency. His contributions continue to shape contemporary management theories and practices.

www.ingramcontent.com/pod-product-compliance
Lightning Source LLC
Chambersburg PA
CBHW071834210526
45479CB00001B/126